Get Ready for Business

Preparing for work

Student Book 1

Andrew Vaughan
& Dorothy E Zemach

MACMILLAN

Contents

Here are some of the companies and characters you will hear about.

ASIA Retailing (AR) Ltd
First in Fashion

Business:	Fashion design & production
Head office:	Singapore
Employees:	45
Offices:	Guangzhou, Tokyo

COMET TECHNOLOGIES
Connecting the world

Business:	Web page design & translation
Head office:	Portland, Oregon, U.S.A.
Employees:	19
Offices:	San Francisco, San Jose

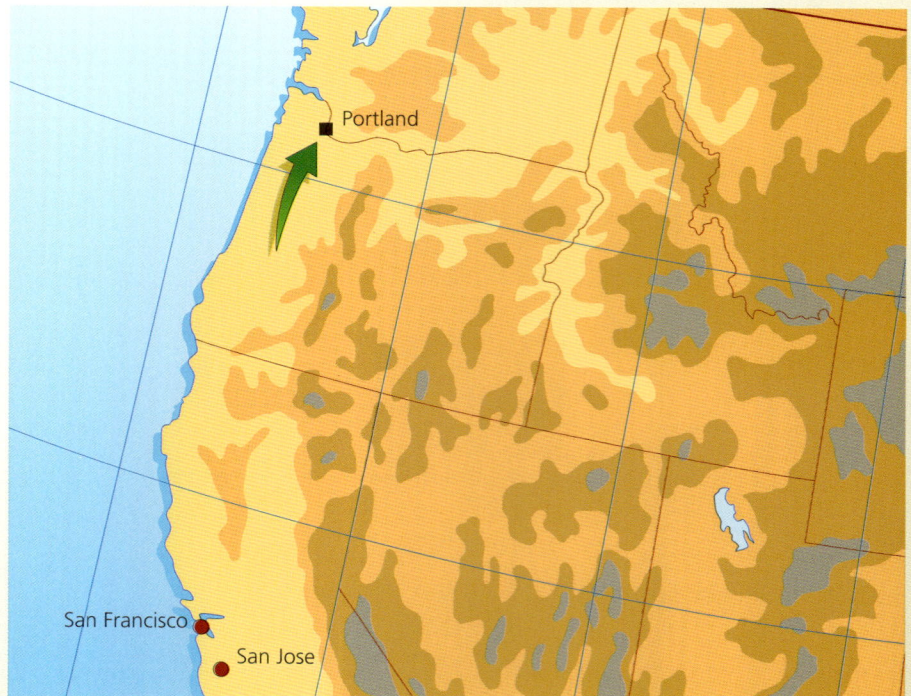

Name:	Hari Kumar
Born:	1975, London, U.K.
Job:	Overseas Marketing Manager
Hobbies:	Windsurfing, Driving, Computer Games

Name:	May Li
Born:	1980, Shanghai, China
Job:	Customer Support
Hobbies:	Cooking, Dancing

Hi, I'm Hari. I work for Asia Retailing in Singapore. I like windsurfing, driving, and computer games.

I'm May Li from Singapore. I work in customer support at Asia Retailing. On weekends I like to cook, and I enjoy dancing with my friends.

Hi there! I'm Sarah, from Oregon. I work for Comet Technologies in Portland. I'm a Web designer. On weekends I like sailing and mountain-biking.

How's it going? I'm Andy. I'm American but I was born in Hong Kong. I work in sales for Comet Technologies. In my free time I like hiking and taking pictures.

Name:	Sarah Cohen
Born:	1982, Portland, Oregon, U.S.
Job:	Web Designer
Hobbies:	Sailing, Cello, Mountain-biking

Name:	Andy Johnson
Born:	1983, Hong Kong
Job:	Sales (Asia)
Hobbies:	Hiking, Photography

Listen and
practice

1   **Describe the picture. Where are the people? What are they doing?**

2   **1.02 Sarah and Hari are meeting. Listen and write T for true or F for false next to each sentence. Then check your answers with a partner.**

    a   They are meeting for the first time. _____

    b   They work for the same company. _____

3   **1.02 Listen again and complete the conversation. Then practice with a partner. Take turns being Sarah and Hari.**

Sarah: Hello. My name's Sarah Cohen. I ___work___ ___for___ Comet Technologies.

Hari: Hi, Sarah. I'm Hari Kumar. I'm _____ Asia Retailing. Nice to _____ you.

Sarah: Nice to meet you too. I'm sorry, I didn't _____ your _____ name.

Hari: It's Kumar. Here – let me _____ you my card.

4   **Now practice the conversation again. Change the information in blue using the names and companies below.**

Josh Brown / Brown Construction

Su-yun Kim / Insung Limited

5   **1.03 What do you think Sarah and Hari will do next? Check (✓) your guesses. Then listen to see if you are correct.**

    a   ☐   Sarah will give Hari her business card.

    b   ☐   Hari will ask for Sarah's phone number.

    c   ☐   They will talk about their companies.

    d   ☐   They will talk about their jobs.

Talking about your job

1 **Look at the chart. It shows questions you can ask about someone's job. Ask and answer the questions with a partner.**

What do you do?	I'm (an engineer). I'm in (R&D).
Who do you work for? Who are you with?	I work for (company name). I'm with (company name).
Where do you work?	I work in (Hong Kong).

2 **Look at the charts. They show ways you can talk about job titles and departments. With a partner or group, add some more.**

		Job title
I'm You're He's / She's	a / an	Web designer / (department) manager / product planner / researcher / sales clerk / administrative assistant / accountant _____ / _____ .

		Department name
I'm You're He's / She's	in	Information Technology (I.T.) / Advertising / Human Resources / Marketing / Purchasing / Sales / Research & Development (R&D) _____ / _____ .

3 **Complete the sentences using words from the charts above.**

a He's ___an accountant.___

b You're _____

c I'm _____

d She's _____

e He's _____

4 🔘 1.04 **Listen to the conversation. Then practice with a partner. Take turns being Amanda and Steve.**

Amanda:	Hello. Are you new here?
Steve:	Yes, I just started on Monday.
Amanda:	Really? That's great. By the way, my name's Amanda Parker. Please call me Mandy. I'm an administrative assistant.
Steve:	Nice to meet you, Mandy. I'm Steve Klein.
Amanda:	Nice to meet you. What do you do, Steve?
Steve:	I'm in Advertising. Well, I'll see you around.
Amanda:	See you.

5 **Now practice the conversation again. Change the information in blue using your own names and information from exercise 2.**

1 **Look at the business card. Take turns reading the numbers and addresses with a partner. Then label the card with words from the box.**

area code   country code   zip code   at   dot   underscore

C☀MET TECHNOLOGIES

Sarah Cohen Web Designer

1256 West Park Lane, Portland, OR 97202

+1 (503) 555-3681

s_cohen@comet.com

Connecting the world

a _____

b _____

c _____

d _____

e _____

f _____

2 🔊 1.05 **Listen to four conversations. Fill in each business card with the missing information.**

a Sebastien Michel

Overseas _____ Manager

FINE FRENCH FOODS

Simply the Best

76 rue St. Martin
Paris, France 75001
+ ___ ___ (1) 55-89-72-36
_____ @aliments_____

c Sayako Kimura
Assistant
_____

Marco Supermarkets

Great Food, Great Prices!

2-14-83 Minami Aoyama
Minato - _____ Tokyo 105-8511
(___ ___) 3578-2111
kimurasay@marco.com

b Max Rosenberg
phone: ___ ___ ___ 555- _____
email: _____

d **UNIVERSITY OF DETROIT**

Detroit, MI ___ ___ ___ ___ ___
(313) 555-0134
alfulani@_____

Dr. Amina Al-Fulani
_____ Professor

👥 Talk business

Student A, turn to page 84.
Student B, turn to page 96.

Starting and ending conversations

1 🔊 1.06 Listen to and read the conversations below. Which one is between friends? Which one is between people meeting for the first time?

Conversation 1

A: Excuse me. Is this seat taken?
B: No, go ahead.
A: Thank you. By the way, my name's Nancy Chen.
B: Nice to meet you, Nancy. I'm Mike Burns. Are you with Global Exports?
A: No, I work for Snappy Snack Foods. I'm in marketing. Here, let me give you my card.
B: Thanks. Here's mine. I'm a sales representative for Golden Palace. We import Chinese food.

Conversation 2

A: Emily! How have you been?
B: Hi, Matt. Really good. Did you hear that I changed jobs?
A: Yeah. Who are you with now?
B: Corporate Training Solutions. I'm in human resources. And you?
A: Oh, I'm still a software developer with Magix. I really like it.
B: Let me give you my new card.

2 Practice the conversations with a partner.

3 Look at these ways to end conversations. Which ones can be used with conversation 1? With conversation 2?

a A: We should get together sometime.
   B: Good idea. I'll call you this weekend, OK?

b A: Well, it was a pleasure meeting you.
   B: Good to meet you too. I'll email you that information you asked about.

c A: Anyway, I'd better get going. Tell your brother I said hi.
   B: I will. See you!

d A: Well, I see someone I need to talk to. It was nice meeting you.
   B: You too. Goodbye.

e A: Well, my train leaves in about an hour. I'd better get going.
   B: I hope we meet again sometime. Have a safe trip.

f A: Oh, look at the time!
   B: Yes, I've got to go. See you around.

4 Practice all of the endings with a partner.

5 Choose an ending to conversation 1 and conversation 2. Then practice the complete conversations.

Viewpoints: Business cards

1 💿 **1.07** **Listen to people from three different countries talking about business cards. Check (✓) the sentences you hear.**

Jane Walker,
Student, England

- [ ] I don't have a business card.
- [ ] Most of my friends have cards.
- [ ] Sometimes people give me their cards.
- [ ] I like **fancy**, colorful cards.
- [ ] I keep business cards in my **pocket**.

Anna Martinez,
Sales manager, Venezuela

- [ ] I give and receive a lot of business cards.
- [ ] My cards are in English.
- [ ] I like **plain** white cards.
- [ ] It's important to treat cards with **respect**.
- [ ] It's OK to write on them.

Michael Yang,
Small business owner, China

- [ ] I have two different business cards.
- [ ] I give my card to everyone I meet.
- [ ] I give and **receive** cards with both hands.
- [ ] I like simple, clear cards.
- [ ] I **organize** them in a small notebook.

2 **Discuss these questions in a small group.**

- Which person is most like you (or people from your country)?
- Do you think business cards are important? Why or why not?
- Do you have a business card?
- How often do you receive business cards? Who do you receive them from, and why?

3 **Look at these business cards in a small group. Which ones do you like? Which ones don't you like? Explain why. Use the vocabulary below and your own ideas.**

(not) easy to read   (not) attractive   (not) simple   (not) interesting

Dan's Auto Repair
In and Out in Less than a week – Guaranteed!

Domestic and Imported Cars
250 W. Saginaw
Flint, MI 48502

Cristina Barela
Travel Time
Specializing in Central and South America

35030 Plaza del Sol
Dallas, TX 75217
(972) 555-6300
http://www.plazatraveltime.com

50% off your next package tour with this card

Magical Max
The Magnificent Magician!

Available for home and office parties
card tricks ★ coin tricks ★ mind reading

Phone: 01986 533045
email: magicalmax@ma

Chelsie Clark, Owner

Happy Paws
Dog Walking and Pet Care

639 Maple Ave.
Ames, IA 50010
(515) 555-2745 (home)
(515) 555-9020 (cell)

Dagmar Karlsson, Ph.D.
Translator
English, French, German, Swedish

115 92 Stockholm
☎ +46-(0)8-2491-3201
✉ dagmar.karlsson@swedtrans.net

Project: Design a business card

In this course, you will create an imaginary company, and also a person who works there. Choose something interesting, because you will add details to your company and your employee as you work through this text.

Activity

In this unit, you will decide basic information about your company and your employee.

---

1 **Discuss the questions below with a partner or small group. They might give you ideas to help you create your company and employee for this course.**

- What kinds of jobs interest you?
- What kind of job might you get in the future?
- What kind of company do you want to work for?
- Do you know anyone with an interesting job? What does he / she do?

---

2 **Write the following information about your company:**

Name of company: _____

Type of business: _____

_____

Draw a picture of your company's logo here: ⟶

---

3 **Now create an employee. Write your employee's name, job title, and contact information on the business card below. Don't forget to add the company name and logo!**

4 **Pretend that you are the employee in exercise 3. Stand up and meet the other employees in your class. Meet as many people as possible.**

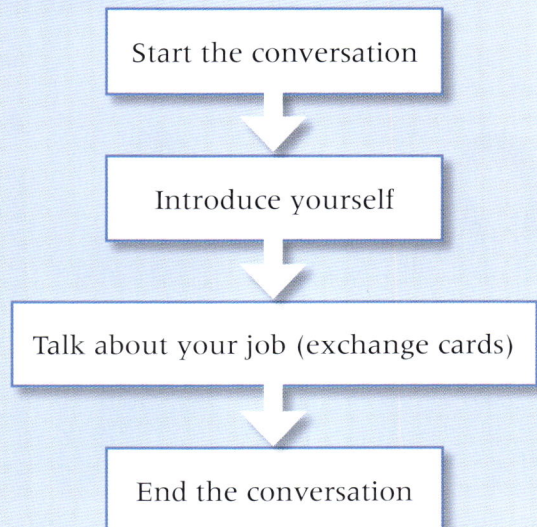

Start the conversation

⬇

Introduce yourself

⬇

Talk about your job (exchange cards)

⬇

End the conversation

2 I start work at 8:30

1 **Describe the picture. What are they doing? What are they saying?**

2 🔊 **1.08 Hari, Sarah, and May are meeting. Listen and write T for true or F for false next to each sentence. Then check your answers with a partner.**

a May and Sarah are meeting for the first time. _____

b Sarah is from the United States. _____

3 🔊 **1.08 Listen again and complete the conversation. Then practice in groups of three. Take turns being Hari, May, and Sarah.**

Hari: Sarah, _____ _____ _____ May Li. May is in customer support. May, _____ _____ Sarah Cohen. Sarah's a designer for Comet Technologies.

May: Nice to meet you, Sarah.

Sarah: Nice to meet you too, May. Where _____ _____ _____ ?

May: I'm from Shanghai, in China. _____ _____ _____ ?

Sarah: I'm from Portland, in the United States.

4 **Now practice the conversation again. Change the information in blue using the information below.**

Kimiko Tatsuda
(Nagoya, Japan)

marketing assistant
Hasegawa Hotels

Maria Lopez
(Mexico City, Mexico)

sales manager
BL Chemicals

Jung-hee Kim
(Incheon, South Korea)

PUSAN PIPE

service engineer
Pusan Pipe Manufacturing

Lek Phikul
(Hat Yai, Thailand)

OUR ASIA

LEK

tour guide
Tour Asia

Ben Poole
(Manchester, England)

product planner
Timson Watches

5 🔘 **1.09 What do you think May will say next? Check (✓) your guesses. Then listen to see if you are correct.**

a ☐ Do you like Singapore?

b ☐ How old are you, Sarah?

c ☐ What do you do, Sarah?

d ☐ Is this your first trip to Singapore?

Conversation strategy

reflecting and reacting

1 Look at the chart. It shows questions you can ask to reflect a question back to the speaker.

| What about you? |
| How about you? |
| And you? |

I'm a student. And you?

2 🔘 **1.10 Listen to the four conversations. How do the speakers reflect the question?**

a _____ you?

b _____ you?

c _____ you?

d _____ you?

3 Ask and answer the questions with a partner.

For example: **A:** *Where were you born?*

B: *I was born in _____ . How about you?*

A: *I was born in _____ .*

a Who is your favorite singer?

b Can you play a musical instrument?

c What kind of movies do you like?

d Do you play any sports?

e Where are you from?

f Do you like fish?

4 Look at the chart. It shows ways you can react to information.

😃	🙂	🙁
Wow!	Really?	That's too bad.
That's amazing!	That's interesting.	Oh no!
That's great!	I see.	I'm sorry to hear that.

🔘 **1.11 Listen and repeat. Try to say the expressions the same way.**

5 Practice with a partner. Take turns reading and reacting. Use the information below and your own ideas.

For example: **A:** *I'm getting married next week!*
B: *That's great!*

a I'm studying French.

c I lost my train pass.

b I went skiing last weekend.

d I have a bad cold.

Describing routines

1 🔊 1.12 Listen to May describe a typical work day. Next to each activity write how often she does these things. Then check your answers with a partner.

every day	once		day
most days	twice	a	week
some days	three times		month
	four times		year

get up at 6:30	a	*every day*
stop for coffee and a muffin	b	
leave home at 7:30	c	
have a morning meeting	d	
eat a sandwich at my desk	e	
study for an hour	f	

Talk business

Student A, turn to page 85.
Student B, turn to page 97.

2 Practice with a partner. Talk about some things you do.

For example: **A:** *Most days I drink coffee in the morning. How about you?*
B: *Some days I drink coffee. But I drink tea three or four times a day!*

1 **Look at the chart. It shows ways you can talk about schedules.**

Preposition	Unit	Examples
on	day	on Monday, on Friday
at	time	at nine o'clock, at 8:30 p.m.
in	month, year, part of day, season	in March, in 2010 in the morning, in spring
from … to …	day, time, month, year	from Monday to Thursday, from 4:00 to 6:00 p.m. from April to June, from 2008 to 2010

2 **Put the correct prepositions in the spaces. Check your answers with a partner.**

a The meeting starts _____ 10:00 a.m.

b _____ Monday _____ Wednesday I work in our head office.

c _____ the afternoon I have a conference call with the U.S.

d I take my vacation _____ August.

e Lunchtime is _____ twelve-fifteen _____ one o'clock.

f Men don't need to wear ties _____ summer.

g I joined this company _____ 2007.

h _____ Monday we have a morning meeting.

3 1.13 **Listen and complete the schedule.**

Hiro Makino: March Business Trip

3/ ___	12:05 p.m.	Shanghai–New York (arrive _____)
3/16	_____ – _____	Inspect Factory Site
3/16	_____	New York–Dallas
3/ ___	9:00 a.m. – 12:00 p.m.	Texas Oil: Presentation
3/17	_____	Dallas–SF
3/17	5:00 p.m. – _____	SF Office: interview Lindsey Cole
3/17	_____	Dinner: Dieter Muller (SF Manager)
3/18	_____	SF–Shanghai (arrive 3/19 9:40 p.m.)

4 **Write true or false statements about Mr. Makino's schedule. Listen to your partner's statements. Are they true or false?**

For example: *Mr. Makino is arriving in Shanghai on March 18th.* False!

a _____

b _____

c _____

Viewpoints: Working hours

1 **Read what these people say about working hours. Answer the questions.**

- How many days a week do most people work in your country?
- Do most people work long hours in your country?
- How much vacation do people get in your country?

Maggie Kirk
Office worker, Australia

I work for a busy **property developer** in Sydney. I travel a lot, so I'm a **telecommuter**. This means I can work from home, a hotel, or anywhere. I go to the office once or twice a month for meetings with my boss. I work a 40-hour week, but I can decide my schedule every day. This is good for me because I have two small children. I have four weeks' **vacation** every year, and I try to take **time off** in summer when my children are out of school.

Soo-hyun Park,
Administrative staff, Korea

I start work at 8:30. I work five days a week for eight hours a day, with one hour off for lunch. When we are busy, I work **overtime**. Sometimes I work on Saturdays. In my first year with the company I had ten vacation days, but now I have 20 days a year. It's difficult for me to take more than four or five days at one time, because my job is very busy. Most people don't use all their vacation days.

Michel DuBois,
Systems engineer, France

In France work-life balance is important. I work a 35-hour week from Monday to Friday. We have a **flexitime** system. I can decide when to come to the office, but I must be there between 10:00 a.m. and 3:00 p.m. In my company there is no overtime. We have five weeks' vacation every year. Many companies in France close for a month in the summer – my company closes for three weeks in August.

2 **What is important to you when you look for a job?**
Rate these items 1–5 (1 = very important, 5 = not important).

	Friendly colleagues	Flexitime	Interesting work	Long vacations	No overtime	Good salary	Telecommuting
Importance							

3 **Talk about your answers in a group.**

For example: **A:** *I think _____ is / are very important. How about you?*
  B: *I don't think _____ is / are important. How about you?*

Project: Describe a work day

Review

Using the information you created in Unit 1, introduce yourself to other class members and ask / answer questions about your job. Don't forget to react, reflect, and end the conversation!

What do you do? *I'm an engineer.* *Let me give you my card.* *I've got to go.*

Who do you work for? *Nice to meet you.* *See you around.* *Goodbye.*

I'm in sales. *And you?* *Really?*

How about you?

Activity

1 For the employee you created in Unit 1, make a schedule for a typical work day.

TIME	PLACE	ACTIVITY

2 Present your information to other class members. When you listen to your classmates, remember to react, reflect, and ask questions.
Begin like this:

This is my work day. From / At _____ I …

3 What does your company do?

Listen and practice

1 **Describe the picture. Where are the people? What are they talking about?**

2 🔊 **1.14 Andy is asking May about Asia Retailing. Listen and circle the correct answer. Ask and answer the questions with a partner.**

a	Was AR established in 1993?	Yes, it was.	No, it wasn't.
b	Is AR's head office in Hong Kong?	Yes, it is.	No, it isn't.
c	Does AR have an office in Nagoya?	Yes, it does.	No, it doesn't.

3 🔊 **1.14 Listen again and complete the conversation. Then practice with a partner. Take turns being Andy and May.**

Andy: Can I ask you some questions about AR?

May: Yes, of course.

Andy: _____ _____ _____ the company?

May: We were established in 1992.

Andy: I see. And _____ _____ _____ head office?

May: In Singapore. We also have offices in Guangzhou and Tokyo.

Andy: _____ _____ people work for AR?

May: We have 45 full-time employees. 35 people work in our head office, and there are ten workers in our other offices.

4 **Now practice the conversation again. Change the names and numbers in blue using the information below.**

Company	Established	Employees	Head Office	Offices
Timson Watches	1835	150	Geneva (120)	London (10), New York (20)
Natural Beauty	1994	670	Milan (350)	New York (120), Hong Kong (200)
Tour Asia	2000	104	Singapore (60)	Beijing (20), Seoul (14), Bangkok (10)
Comet Technology	2003	19	Portland (10)	San Francisco (5), San Jose (4)

5 🎵 **1.15** **What do you think Andy will ask next? Check (✓) your guesses. Then listen to see if you are correct.**

a ☐ He will ask May where she lives.

b ☐ He will ask about AR's customers.

c ☐ He will ask May about her job.

d ☐ He will ask May for her telephone number.

Asking about company background

1 **Look at the chart. It shows questions you can ask about a company.**

What		does	your company	do?
Where		is	your head office?	
When		was	the company	established?
How many	offices employees	do	you	have?

2 🎵 **1.16** **Listen and complete the notes. Then check your answers with a partner.**

a

Batang Corp.
Established:
Head Office: **Kuala Lumpur**
Offices:
Employees:
Business: imports and
exports goods

c

BL Chemicals
Established:
Head Office:
Offices: **80**
Employees:
Business: produces plastic
goods

b

Insung Ltd.
Established:
Head Office:
Offices:
Employees: **1,200**
Business: supplies foodstuffs

d

Brown Construction
Established: **1913**
Head Office:
Offices:
Employees:
Business: designs and builds
roads and bridges

3 Look at the examples of long and short answers below.
Then ask and answer the questions about the companies in exercise 2.

When was _____ established?	It was established in (2003). / In (2003).
How many employees does _____ have?	It has (750) employees. / (750).
Where is the head office of _____ ?	The head office is in (Seoul). / In Seoul.
How many offices does _____ have?	It has (four) offices. / (four).

4 Now ask and answer questions about Seki Steel with a partner.

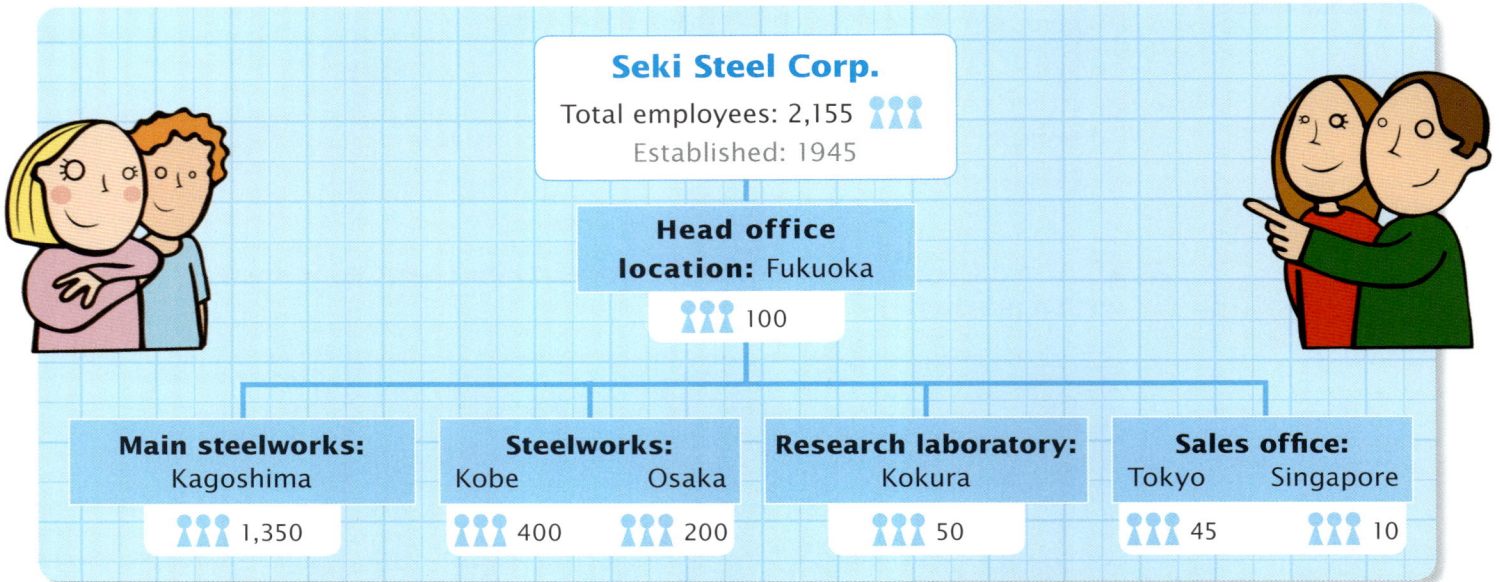

Seki Steel Corp.

Total employees: 2,155

Established: 1945

Head office location: Fukuoka

100

Main steelworks:	Steelworks:		Research laboratory:	Sales office:	
Kagoshima	Kobe	Osaka	Kokura	Tokyo	Singapore
1,350	400	200	50	45	10

5 Practice with a partner. Student A, give an answer.
Student B, ask the question.

For example: **A:** *Two.*

B: *How many steelworks does Seki Steel have?*

B: *In Fukuoka.*

A: *Where is the head office of Seki Steel?*

Conversation strategy

asking for repetition and spelling

Talk business

Student A, turn to page 86.

Student B, turn to page 98.

1 Look at the chart. It shows ways you can ask someone to repeat or spell what he or she has said.

I'm sorry,	can you repeat that? can you say that again? can you spell that?	
	can you repeat / spell	your telephone number? the address? your family name?

2 Practice with a partner. Take turns asking the questions.

Look at these ways you can talk about what companies do.

> AR **designs** clothes for the fashion industry.
>
> Comet **provides** design and translation of web pages.

1 🔊 1.17 **Listen and draw a line from the company to the product. Then write the correct words from the box on the lines. You can use some words twice.**

builds   develops   manufactures   sells   designs   produces

a   Brown Construction   *designs and builds*
b   Amazon   _____
c   BL Chemicals   _____
d   Capcom   _____
e   Nisco   _____

roads and bridges

video games

books and CDs

plastic goods

integrated circuits

2 **Complete the following sentences, using companies you know. Talk about the companies with a partner.**

a   _____ sells _____ .
b   _____ makes _____ .
c   _____ .
d   _____ .
e   _____ .

3 **Ask and answer *yes / no* questions with a partner using the information in exercises 1 and 2.**

> Q: Does _____ sell _____ ?   A: Yes, it does. / No, it doesn't.
>
> Q: Does _____ build _____ ?   A: Yes, it does. / No, it doesn't.

Viewpoints: What kind of company?

1 Answer these questions for yourself. Write T for true or F for false next to each sentence. Compare your answers with a partner.

   a I want to work for a big company.

   b I want to work in a foreign country.

   c I want to stay at one company for a long time.

2 🔘 1.18 Listen to these people talk about their companies. Match the person with what they say.

☐ My company develops medicines.   ☐ I like working for a big company.   ☐ I work for a small family company.

a Neil Parker, Pharmacist, U.S.

b George Weber, Electrical engineer, Germany

c Emiko Yamaguchi, Banker, Japan

☐ Everyone is friendly and I enjoy my job.   ☐ We have offices in New York, London and Tokyo.   ☐ I need to improve my English!

3 Look at these types of industries. Can you think of any more?

Raw materials	Manufacturing		Services	
Farming	Construction	IT & Software	Banking	Hospitality
Fishing	Electronics	Pharmaceuticals	Education	News media
Mining	the automotive industry		Entertainment	Tourism
	the chemical industry		Health care	Transportation

4 What kind of industry do you want to work in? Talk about the industries with a small group. Use some of these adjectives or other words you know.

creative   difficult   exciting   interesting   challenging   well-paid

For example: *I want to work in (the chemical industry) because it's interesting. How about you?*

I want to work in (tourism) because I like to travel. How about you?

Project: Describe your company

Review

What do you do?

How about you?

I'm sorry, can you spell that?

Where do you work?

I'm sorry, could you repeat that?

Nice to meet you.

Who do you work for?

Where is your head office?

Using the information you created in Units 1 and 2, introduce yourself to other class members and ask / answer questions about your job and company. Don't forget to ask for repetition and / or spelling if you need to!

Activity

1 **Make an information sheet about your company. Include information on when you were established, where your head office is, how many offices or factories you have, how many people work there, etc.**

Company name and logo:

Company information:

Established:

Employees:

Head Office:

_____

_____

_____

2 **Stand up and interview other people to get information about their companies.**
Begin like this: *May I ask you some questions about your company?*
Yes, of course.

4 How do you like your job?

Listen and practice

1 **Describe the picture. Where are they? What are they doing?**

2 🔘 1.19 **Andy is talking with Sarah. Listen and check (✓) whether he likes or dislikes these things.**

		likes	dislikes
a	Portland	☐	☐
b	parks	☐	☐
c	rain	☐	☐

3 🔘 1.19 **Listen again and complete the conversation. Then practice with a partner. Take turns being Andy and Sarah.**

Andy: Hi, Sarah. How's it going?

Sarah: Oh, hi, Andy. Not bad. So, _____ do you _____ Portland?

Andy: It's pretty nice. Well, _____ , it rains a lot …

Sarah: Yeah, it does. That's why there are so many _____ parks here.

Andy: That's true. They're _____ . But I _____ _____ hiking in the rain!

4 🔘 1.20 **Andy talked about some things he didn't like. How will Sarah respond? Check (✓) your guesses. Then listen to see if you are correct.**

a ☐ She will agree with him.

b ☐ She will talk about something she doesn't like.

c ☐ She will suggest some things for him to do.

d ☐ She will get angry.

1 To make small talk, people often share their likes and dislikes. Look at the chart. It shows ways you can do this. Practice with a partner. Take turns reading the sentences.

	like enjoy	my job. taking business trips.
I	don't mind	our cafeteria.
	don't like can't stand	waiting in line. commuting.

2 Talk to your partner about some other activities that you like or dislike.

For example: **A:** *I like baseball. How about you?*

B: *Me too. I like baseball.*

Or

Really? I can't stand baseball.

3 Look at the words in the box below. Are they positive or negative? Put them into the chart. Then discuss your choices with a partner, and add some more words to each list.

✓ attractive	challenging	difficult	exciting	fun
✓ boring	confusing	easy	frustrating	interesting

positive	**negative**
attractive	boring

4 Look at ways you can give more information about likes and dislikes. Practice with a partner. Take turns being A and B.

A: How do you like your job? *(question)*	**B:** I love it. **It's great**. It's OK. **It's a little boring**. Actually, **it's frustrating**.
A: I like our new uniforms. *(statement)*	**B:** Yeah, me too. **They're attractive**. Really? Actually, **I can't stand them!**

5   **Practice with a partner. Student A: read a question or statement. Student B: respond. Take turns asking and responding in different ways.**

questions	statements
How do you like your new job?	I don't like long vacations.
How do you like living here?	I like working on weekends.
How do you like the cafeteria food?	I like our new computers.
(your own idea)	(your own idea)

Making suggestions

1   💿 **1.21 When someone talks about something he or she doesn't like, you can make a suggestion. Listen to the sentences in the chart. Then practice reading each sentence to a partner.**

You should	ask your boss for a day off.
Why don't you	ask your boss for a day off?
I recommend	asking your boss for a day off.
How about	asking your boss for a day off?

2   💿 **1.22 Listen to four employees talking about their problems. What suggestion does someone make? Number them in order a–d as you hear them. There are two extra suggestions.**

- ☐ I recommend taking an earlier train.
- ☐ Why don't you bring your own lunch?
- ☐ You should talk to your manager.
- ☐ Why don't you ask for more training?
- ☐ You should look for a new job.
- ☐ How about reading the manual?

👥 Talk business

Student A, turn to page 87.

Student B, turn to page 99.

3 Work in groups of three. Make suggestions for these situations. Spend five minutes on each situation. One person writes down the suggestions. Then share your ideas with the class.

- My parents said I can choose my own birthday present this year. What should I ask for?
- I want to make some friends in other countries.
- I have a one-week vacation. I want to go somewhere interesting.

For example: *Why don't you go to Hawaii?*

Language can be polite or impolite, but your tone of voice – how you sound when you say something – is also very important.

1 🎧 1.23 Listen to these sentences said two different ways. The first way is polite; the second way is impolite.

> Why don't you ask for a day off?
> How about reading the manual?

2 🎧 1.24 Listen to the conversations. Pay attention to the speakers' tone of voice. Which responses sound polite? Which don't? Check (✓) the appropriate box.

> It's really easy!

		polite	impolite
a	**A:** I don't know how to use this fax machine. **B:** It's really easy.	☐	☐
b	**A:** I feel exhausted! **B:** Why don't you sit down?	☐	☐
c	**A:** I don't have the company's phone number. **B:** How about looking it up online?	☐	☐
d	**A:** How can I get to the restaurant? **B:** How about taking a taxi?	☐	☐

3 Practice the conversations with a partner. Student B should first try to sound impolite. Practice again, and student B should try to sound polite. Take turns being A and B.

Viewpoints: Corporate culture

1 **Read what these employees from around the world say about the corporate culture in their companies.**

Marcus Bodine,
Software designer, U.S.

I work for a software company. We work hard, with a lot of overtime, but we have fun, too – for example, on Fridays, we wear **casual** clothes, like jeans and a Hawaiian shirt. Sometimes my group goes out for pizza together. And we always have a big company picnic in the summer. People bring their families, and we play softball.

Alma Hansson,
Accounts manager, Sweden

I started working last year for an IT company. It's easy for me to talk to my co-workers and my managers. My manager wants me to give my **opinion**. In Sweden, we don't talk about our families or hobbies at work. I don't usually talk about my job with my family. We don't mix our work lives and our personal lives.

Hassan Zouabi,
Civil servant, Egypt

I work in a government office in Cairo. I **greet** everyone in my office each day. Respect, good **manners**, and relationships between people are important! I talk and socialize with my co-workers while I work. Our managers **praise** the workers often. This makes us want to work harder.

2 **Discuss these questions with a group.**

- Which company or companies seem similar to ones in your country? Which are different?
- Which work customs do you think you'd like? Are there any you wouldn't like?
- Imagine you work for a company that you like very much. Tell your group three things that make it a good company to work for.

Project: Conversation role-play

Review

Work in groups of three or four. Take turns making statements about your classmates' companies and employees. They will tell you if you are correct or not.

For example: **A:** *Your employee often works overtime.*

B: *That's correct!*

C: *Your company manufactures cars.*

B: *Sorry, that's not quite right. Actually, it* **paints** *cars.*

Activity

1   Complete the following word web with information about your employee's likes and dislikes, e.g., meeting people; writing reports; long meetings.

likes

dislikes

2   Work in pairs or small groups. Talk about your employee's likes and dislikes. Listen to your classmates' descriptions. React appropriately and make suggestions where possible.

Review: Units 1–4

1 Sentence scramble

Unscramble the sentences. Then number them in the correct order to make a conversation. Then practice with a partner.

interesting wow Bangkok that's !

_____ _____ !

office head in our Bangkok is .

_____ _____ .

company old is how the ?

  1 _____ ?

where head office your is ?

_____ _____ ?

1956 were established we in .

_____ _____ .

2 Crossword

Look at the clues and complete the puzzle.

Across: 1 I can't do this puzzle.
It's too d_____

3 I need to learn many new things in
my job. It's c_____ but I enjoy it.

5 I don't mind studying English.
Sometimes it's i_____

6 I can't stand housework.
It's so b_____

Down: 2 I like this puzzle a lot.
It's f_____

4 I enjoy visiting new places.
It's e_____

3 Face-to-face

Use these cards to introduce yourself to a partner.

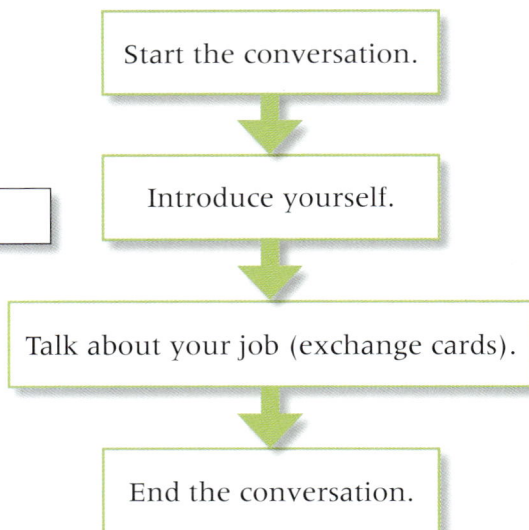

Timson Watches
Geneva, London, New York

Ben Poole
Product Planner
Tel: 7858-465-9979
Email: poole-b@timsonwatches.com

Pusan Pipe Mfg.

Jung-hee Kim   Service Engineer

Kim_jh@pusanpipe.co.kr   051-726-7853

Start the conversation.

↓

Introduce yourself.

↓

Talk about your job (exchange cards).

↓

End the conversation.

4 Matching pairs

Connect A and B to make questions.

	A		B
1	Can you	a	do you work for?
2	Where	b	Nissan build cars?
3	Why don't	c	was Amazon established?
4	How do you	d	about you?
5	Who	e	repeat that?
6	How	f	do you do?
7	When	g	offices do you have?
8	How about	h	you study harder?
9	Does	i	like your job?
10	How many	j	do you work?
11	What	k	taking a rest?

5 Happy and sad

🔘 1.25 😀 😊 😟

Listen to these five people. React (e.g. "Wow!", "Really?", "That's too bad") when you hear the beep.

6 Daily life

Complete the information for yourself. Describe your routine to a partner. When you listen, remember to reflect / react.

Every day		wake up at _____ .
		eat _____ for breakfast.
Most days	I	_____ .
		_____ .
Some days		_____ .
		go to sleep at _____ .

7 Which preposition?

Put the correct prepositions in the spaces.

I met my friend _____ 12 o' clock _____ Saturday. _____ 12:30 _____ three we went bowling. _____ the evening we went to karaoke. Next week _____ the 14ᵗʰ we are going hiking. _____ summer we are going on vacation to Europe together.

8 Company profile

Ask and answer questions about Natural Beauty with a partner. Then give an answer and ask someone to make the question.

Natural Beauty:
Established: 1994

Offices:

Milan (head office)
👥👥👥 350

New York	**Hong Kong**
👥👥👥 120	👥👥👥 200

9 What's the matter?

🔘 1.26 **Jill has many problems. Listen and make a suggestion when you hear the beep. You can use the ideas here or make your own. Remember to sound polite!**

go to the bank
drink some water
take a rest
take some medicine
eat lunch
call the help desk

5 Can I take a message?

Welcome to
ASIA Retailing
Customer order process

Reception

1 Describe the picture. Where are they? What are they saying?

2 🔘 **1.27** Listen to the telephone call. Write T for true or F for false next to each sentence. Then check your answers with a partner.

a Andy wants to speak to Hari. _____   **b** Hari is out of the office. _____

3 🔘 **1.27** Listen again and complete the conversation. Then practice with a partner. Take turns being the receptionist and Andy.

Receptionist: Asia Retailing. How can I help you?
Andy: Hello, can I _____ _____ Hari Kumar please?
Receptionist: Can I have _____ _____ please?
Andy: It's Andy Johnson from Comet Technologies.
Receptionist: I'm sorry, I can't hear you. Can you repeat that?
Andy: Yes, of course, Andy Johnson from Comet Technologies.
Receptionist: Thank you, Mr. Johnson. I'll transfer your call.
Hari: Hello, _____ _____ Hari _____ .

4 Now practice the conversation again. Change the names and numbers in blue using the information below.

Caller	Receptionist	Receiver
Mary Chan (Pacific Finance)	Tour Asia	Lek Phikul
Jeff Howes (C&F Stores)	Timson Watches	Ben Poole
Mike Burns (Golden Palace)	Snappy Snack Foods	Nancy Chen

5 🔘 **1.28 What do you think Andy will say next? Check (✓) your guesses. Then listen to see if you are correct.**

a ☐ How are you?

b ☐ Hari, can I meet you today?

c ☐ Hari, this is Andy Johnson. How are you?

d ☐ I'm calling to ask if we can meet today.

Answering the phone

1 Look at the chart. It shows ways you can answer the phone.

	morning.		Can I help you?
Good	afternoon.	(Comet Technologies).	How can I help you?
	evening.		May I help you?

2 🔘 **1.29 Listen and repeat what you hear. Try to use the same intonation.**

a Good morning. Northwest Media Services … ?

b Good evening. Corporate Training Solutions … ?

c Good afternoon. Aztec Coffee … ?

d Good morning. Marco Supermarkets … ?

Conversation strategy

controlling language

1 Write the questions (a–e) next to the correct category to show different ways of controlling language. Check your answers with a partner.

a Can you speak more loudly?

b Can you repeat that?

c How do you spell (that)?

d Can you speak more slowly?

e Can you say that again?

Speed _____   _____ Volume

Controlling language

Repetition *Can you repeat that?* _____ Spelling

_____

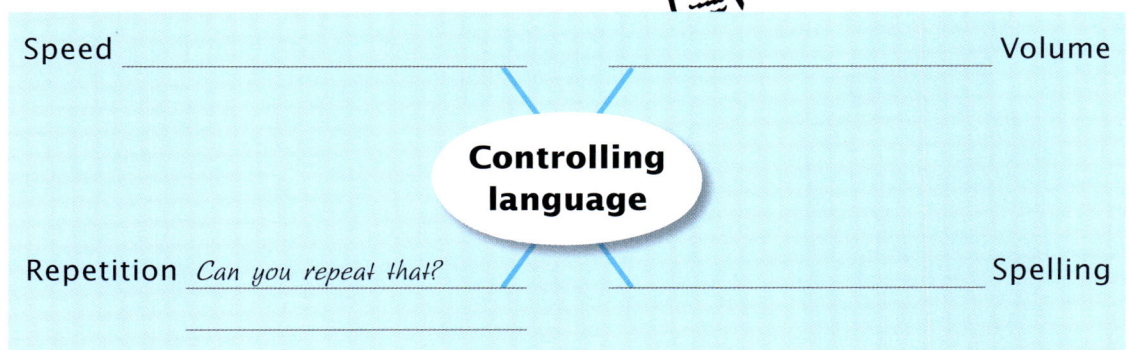

(**Note:** English speakers sometimes say *Speak louder* in informal situations.)

2 🔘 **1.30 Listen to four conversations and write the letter (a–d) of the question you hear.**

a _____   b _____   c _____   d _____

1 🔘 **1.31 Listen to the conversation. Then practice with a partner.**

Receptionist: Ashwell Transportation. How can I help you?

Caller: Can I speak to Kevin Aston, please? This is Tim Horowitz.

Receptionist: Just a moment, please. … Hello? I'm sorry but Mr. Aston is in a meeting. Can I take a message?

2 Practice the conversation with a different partner. Change the information in blue using your real names and the information below.

out of the office
on a business trip
on vacation
out sick
not at his desk
on another line

3 Look at the chart. It shows phrases you can use for messages.

Can I take a message?	Yes.	Please ask her to call me back. Please tell her I called.
	No,	thank you. I'll call back later. that's OK. Thank you.

4 Practice with a partner. Use this conversation map.

Caller:	Receptionist:
"Ring, ring."	Give company name.
Ask to speak to Ms. …	Ask caller to repeat that. Ask caller to speak more slowly.
Repeat slowly.	Ask for caller's name.
Give name.	Ask caller to speak louder.
Give name again.	Ask caller to wait. Tell caller that Ms. / Mr. … is (not there). Offer to take a message.
Respond.	

5 🔘 **1.32 Listen and complete the messages below.**

a

2:40
Tom,
Margaret _____ from _____
Corporation called. Can you call her
back after _____ ?
Her number is 090 - _____ -
_____ .

Hisako.

b

To: Josh Brown

Date: March 22ⁿᵈ   **Time:** 09:30

Message:

Taken by: Maria

c *While you were out:*

Caller: Manuel _____
            of Aztec Coffee

Tel: _____

☐ **Please call back**   ☐ **No message**
☐ **Will call you back**   ☐ **Other**

Message:
José _____ from the Philippines called.
He will call you back _____ .

Received by: Heena   **Time:** 10:25

d **From:** Alison Chen
Date: September 29ᵗʰ, 2009
To: Peter Weybridge
Subject: <Important> Telephone Call

Peter,

Ms. _____ from _____ called this morning.
Can you call her back as soon as possible?

Her number is __01__   __87__ _____

Regards,
Alison

Ending a call

1 **Look at these ways of ending a phone call.**

Receiver	Caller
a I'll give (her) your message.	
b Thank you for calling.	**e** Thank you.
c Thank you for your call.	**f** Goodbye.
d Goodbye.	

Talk business

Student A, turn to page 88.
Student B, turn to page 100.

2 🔘 **1.32 Listen again to the conversations in exercise 5. Which phrases do they use to end the calls? Write the letters in the boxes for each conversation.**

a ☐ ☐ ☐ ☐   **c** ☐ ☐ ☐ ☐
b ☐ ☐ ☐ ☐   **d** ☐ ☐ ☐ ☐

Viewpoints: Cell phones

1 **Answer these questions for yourself. Compare your answers with other class members.**

- Do you have a cell phone?
- What do people in your country use cell phones for?

2 💿 1.33 **Listen to people from three different countries talking about their cell phones. Check (✓) the sentences you hear.**

Hye-won Park,
Sales clerk, Korea

- [ ] I send 20 to 30 **text messages** a day.
- [ ] I don't use it at the office.
- [ ] I can use my phone as a train pass.
- [ ] It's not **convenient**.

Melissa Golding,
Student, U.S.

- [ ] My parents call me every week.
- [ ] I don't **text** much – it's easier and cheaper to email.
- [ ] I feel safe if I'm driving.
- [ ] I hate it when people use their phones in restaurants.

Thomas Mueller,
Engineer, Germany

- [ ] The company uses it to contact me.
- [ ] I like to play games.
- [ ] I also read the news on the Internet.
- [ ] I use the **alarm** when I stay in hotels.

3 **Discuss these questions in a small group.**

- Which person is most like you (or people from your country)?
- Are there any rules in your country about where you cannot use cell phones?
- Do people in your country use cell phones on buses and trains? In restaurants?

4 **What functions are important to you when you buy or use a cell phone? Rate these items 1–5 (1 = very important, 5 = not important). Talk about your answers in a group.**

Color		Camera		Music	
Size		Internet		Games	
Cost		TV		Text messages	
Alarm		Calculator		Schedule	
(Your idea)					

Project: Telephone calls

Review

Write three true sentences about your company on a piece of paper. Do NOT write your company's name. Your teacher will collect the papers, mix them up, and give you someone else's paper. Find the person who created the company by asking questions.

For example:

A: *Is your head office in Paris?*   **B:** *Yes, it is.*

A: *Was your company established in 1879?*   **B:** *No, sorry, it wasn't.*

When you find the person who wrote the paper, return it to him or her.

Activity

1   **Make phone calls and leave messages for someone to call you back. Use the business card you made in Unit 1 and information from other people's cards.**

Before you begin, complete this information about the people you will call:

Call 1

Name:	
Company:	

Call 2

Name:	
Company:	

2   **Now receive two phone calls and take messages. Use the forms below. (You are the receptionist for your company.)**

Message for:

Caller:

Company:

Tel:

☐ Please call back   ☐ No message

☐ Will call you back   ☐ Other

Message:

Received by: Time:

Message for:

Caller:

Company:

Tel:

☐ Please call back   ☐ No message

☐ Will call you back   ☐ Other

Message:

Received by: Time:

6 | Which ones should we order?

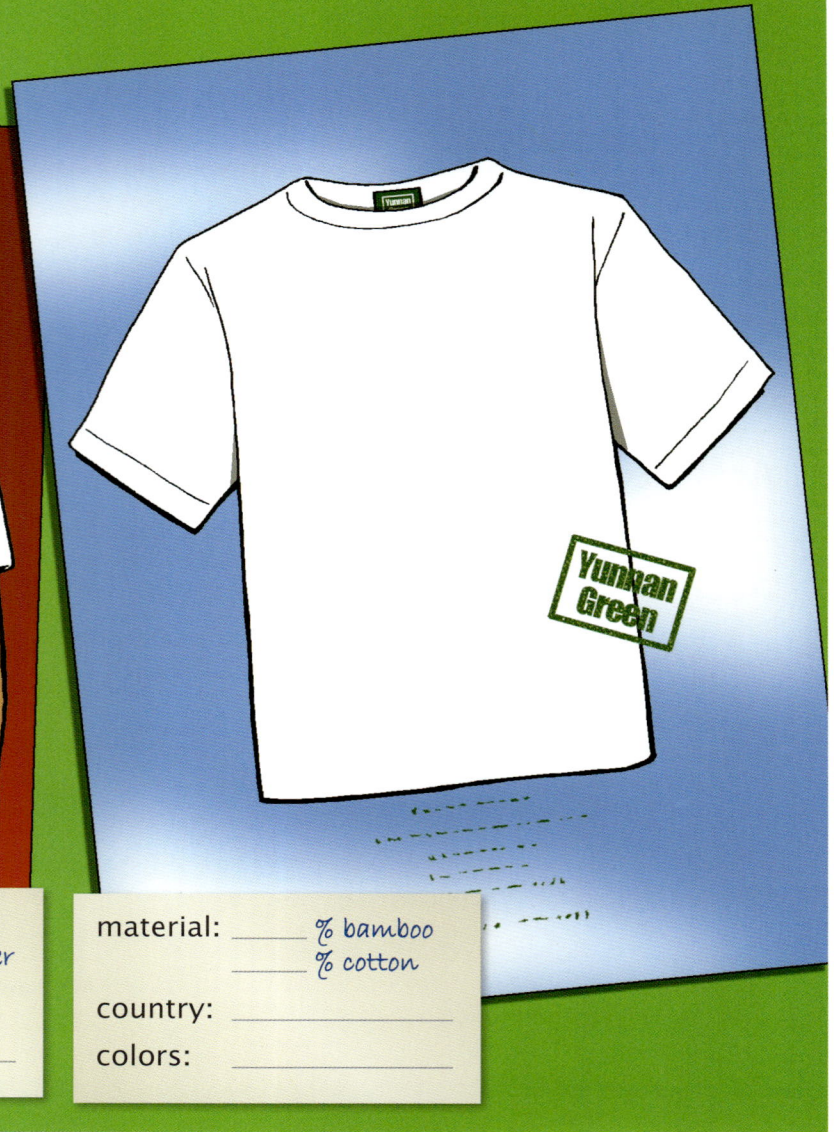

material: _____ % cotton
_____ % polyester

country: Indonesia

colors: _____

material: _____ % bamboo
_____ % cotton

country: _____

colors: _____

1 **Describe the pictures. What do they show?**

2 🔘 1.34 **Hari is giving a presentation to the Purchasing Department. Listen and check (✓) which T-shirts he prefers.**

☐ Java Gear

☐ Yunnan Green

3 🔘 1.34 **Listen again and complete the brochures with the correct information. Check your answers with a partner.**

4 🔘 1.35 **How else will Hari compare the two companies? What will he talk about? Check (✓) your guesses. Then listen to see if you are correct.**

a ☐ price   **b** ☐ size   **c** ☐ quality   **d** ☐ style

1 Look at the chart. It shows words you can use to describe products. Complete the chart with a partner. Can you think of any more words?

	~er / ~ier	more ~ (than)
cheap	cheaper	
compact		more compact
easy	easier	
energy-efficient		
fast		
heavy		
light		
new		
reliable		

2 Look at the chart again and talk with a partner. When do you add ~er to a word? ~ier? When do you use *more*? Note these exceptions:

good ~ better   bad ~ worse   fun ~ more fun

3 Read the conversation with a partner.

A: This looks like a great camera. And it's really cheap.

B: Yeah. But I think that one is cheaper. It's also more compact.

A: Hmm. You're right. That's important.

4 Now practice the conversation again. Change the products and the descriptions in blue using the ideas below.

a camera
light; compact

b software package
fast; new

c cell phone
energy-efficient;
easy to use

d video game
fun; challenging

e jacket
attractive; cheap

f shredder
compact; reliable

g sandwich
cheap; delicious

h scooter
reliable;
energy-efficient

1 **Match the words and phrases with their definitions.**

a buy one, get one free __3__

b coupon _____

c a 10% discount; 10% off _____

d free shipping _____

e money-back guarantee _____

f on sale _____

1 When you order something, you only pay for the item. You don't pay any mailing costs.

2 A product costs 10% less than it usually does.

3 If you buy one product, you get another one without paying any more money.

4 If you don't like the product, you can return it and the store will return your money.

5 A product costs less money than it usually does.

6 A piece of paper that promises you can pay less money or get some money back (a refund).

2 🔘 **1.36** **Listen and complete the advertisements.**

a

| Home | Classes | Times | Gym | Facilities |

Do you need to get in _____ before summer? Come to Gym of the Stars!

_____ with our top trainers! Daily dance and martial arts _____ help you lose weight and look your _____ – and have _____ !

All of our classes have a _____ .

If you're not happy, we'll give you a full _____ .

Special! ·- - - - - - - - - - - - - - - - ✂ - -

Print this _____ to get a _____ on our diet drinks and vitamins.

Order online and receive _____ shipping.

Talk business

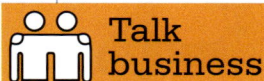

Student A, turn to page 89.
Student B, turn to page 101.

b

Total Fitness

When you're _____ about your health, you're ready for Total Fitness!

Work with a fitness instructor to get _____ results. You'll look and _____ better. Sign up with a friend, and you'll each get _____ off the first month's fee.

Pay for a one-year membership and get _____ !

1 🔊 1.37 **Listen to the two conversations between a sales clerk and a customer. Which one is more polite? Why?**

Conversation 1

A: How do you like this printer?

B: Well, it's kind of large, don't you think?

A: Hmmm. But it's easy to use.

B: I don't know. It's also not very energy-efficient.

Conversation 2

A: How do you like this watch?   B: It's too small.

A: Hmmm. But it's attractive.   B: It's also not cheap.

2 **Practice Conversation 1 with a partner. Underline the phrases in the first conversation that soften the expression, to make it less direct. Add those phrases to Conversation 2. Then practice with a partner.**

3 **Look at the chart. It shows ways that you can soften your language.**

instead of *too*	instead of *not*	At the beginning of a sentence		At the end of a sentence
a bit	not very	Well…	To be honest…	…don't you think?
kind of	not really	Actually…	I don't know.	
rather	not so			

4 🔊 1.38 **Listen to these conversations comparing products. Write down the softening language they use.**

a _____   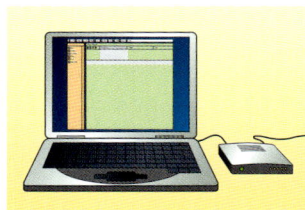    b _____

5 **Talk about these products with a partner.**

expensive, fast, energy-efficient

small, cheap, difficult-to-use

expensive, fashionable, practical

heavy, compact, expensive

Viewpoints: Advertising

1 Read what these people from around the world say about advertisements.

Helen Curtis,
Nurse, England

I'm annoyed by most ads. I don't like ads **interrupting** radio or TV programs. That's why I mostly watch the BBC, which doesn't have any ads. These days, magazines seem to be mostly ads! Even some articles are really just trying to sell you a product. I'm **especially annoyed** by Internet ads. When I'm trying to read a website, I don't like large **flashing** ads for some product I'm not interested in.

Ayako Awano,
Designer, Japan

Actually, I like a lot of TV ads. In Japan, companies never compare themselves directly to another company or criticize their **competitors**. So the ads focus on giving you a good impression of the product and the company. Many ads on TV today are funny or clever. They use a lot of attractive **images**, popular music, and celebrities. In fact, sometimes the ads are better than the programs!

Jim Wright,
Student, U.S.

I don't pay much attention to TV ads, so they don't **bother** me. I'm not impressed by **celebrity endorsements**, though – I don't believe a car is better because someone famous drives it. I look at Internet ads sometimes. It's a good way to find special offers, coupons, and discounts. I don't mind ads if they save me money.

2 Discuss these questions in a group.

- Which person is most like you?
- What kinds of ads annoy you? What kinds of ads do you like?
- How often do you see ads? Where do you see them?
- What do you think about celebrity endorsements? What famous people advertise products that you know about? Have you ever bought any of those products?

Project: Advertise your company

Review

Look at the messages you took in Unit 5 (page 37). Return the calls like this:

A: Hello, (*B's name*). This is (*your name*) from (*your company*).
I'm returning your call from (*Tuesday*). What can I do for you?

B: Oh, yes, hi, (*A's name*). I wanted to *talk to you about / ask you about …*

Activity

1 **Create an advertisement for your company's product or service.
Choose ONE of these options:**

- Write the script for a television or radio ad.
- Draw an ad for a magazine, newspaper, or website.
- Your idea:

2 **Plan your ad here. Discuss your ideas with a partner, and complete the notes.
Then use a separate sheet of paper to create your ad or write your script.**

type of ad (Web, radio, etc.)

words to describe the product or service

special offers (discount, coupon, etc.)

other ideas (celebrity endorsement,
comparison with another product, etc.)

3 **Work in small groups or with the whole class. Take turns displaying or reading
your ads.**

4 **Say something you remember about other companies' products and services. Say if
you would use them or not. If not, say why – softly!**

For example: *I'd buy Crystal Springs Mineral Water because it's refreshing.*
I'd hire Snow White's Cleaning Services because they're reliable and fast.
I'm not sure I'd buy Maki's Sushi. It's a bit expensive.

1 **Describe the pictures. Where are they? What are they doing?**

2 🔊 **1.39 Listen to the telephone call. Write T for true or F for false next to each sentence. Then check your answers with a partner.**

a Sarah wants to meet May next week. _____

b May is busy on Tuesday afternoon. _____

3 🔊 **1.39 Listen again and complete the conversation. Then practice with a partner. Take turns being Sarah and May.**

Sarah: Hi May, this is Sarah from Comet. How are you?

May: Hi Sarah! I'm fine, thanks. How are you?

Sarah: I'm fine. Listen, _____ _____ to ask if we can meet this week.

May: Sure, _____ _____ _____ my schedule. When is good for you?

Sarah: _____ _____ _____ on Tuesday at ten?

May: Let me see. No, sorry _____ _____ _____ . I'm free in the afternoon. How about two-thirty?

Sarah: Two-thirty is fine.

4 **Now practice the conversation again. Change the information in blue using your real names and the information below.**

Caller	Receiver	
on Wednesday at three	in the morning	eleven
on the 25th	on the 26th	four o'clock
tomorrow at nine	on Tuesday	nine-thirty
Friday evening	in the afternoon	three-thirty

5 1.40 **What do you think Sarah will say next? Check (✓) your guesses. Then listen to see if you are correct.**

a ☐ She will ask where they will meet.

b ☐ She will repeat the day and time.

c ☐ She will tell May why she wants to meet.

d ☐ She will ask May for her email address.

Making a telephone call

1 **Look at the chart. It shows ways you can begin a telephone call.**

Hello, … Hello, this is … Hello, my name is …	Can I speak to	Mr. / Ms. .... , please? the sales manager, please? room service, please?	
	I'm calling to I'd like to	change confirm order	(my reservation). (our meeting time). (some flowers).
	I'm calling about	(our meeting tomorrow).	
		(your email).	
		(my reservation).	
	I'm returning your call.		

2 1.41 **Listen and connect the receiver with the caller and the purpose / subject.**

Receiver	Caller	Purpose / Subject
a Toni's Pizza	Mario Fera	Make a reservation
b Jaidev Singh	Junji Tanaka	Meeting time
c Westwood Hotel	Josh Brown	Order food
d José Reina	Rachel Carson	Returning a call

3 **Practice making calls with a partner using the information below. Take turns being the receiver and the caller.**

Receiver	Caller
Grand Hotel Receptionist	Call the Grand Hotel to change your reservation.
Bill Smith	Call Bill Smith to change your meeting time.
Maria Vega	Call Maria Vega to return her call.
Sunset Holidays	Call Sunset Holidays to confirm your reservation.

1 **Look at the chart. It shows ways you can check information or confirm that you understand what someone has said.**

Let me confirm. Let me repeat that.	Your number is … You said … You want to change … Thursday at six o'clock.	Is that right?

2 🔊 1.42 **Listen to the call. Follow this conversation map.**

Caller:		Receptionist:
"Ring, ring."	→	Give the company name. Offer to help.
Ask to speak to …	→	Ask for caller's name.
Give your name.		Ask the caller to spell his / her family name.
Spell your family name.		Ask the caller to wait. Tell the caller that Ms. / Mr. … is (out of the office). Offer to take a message.
Ask him / her to call you back.		
Give the telephone number.		Ask the caller for their telephone number.
Repeat telephone number.		Ask the caller to speak more slowly.
		Check information (telephone number).
Agree.		
		Check information (name, number, message).
Agree.		
End the call.		End the call.

Talk business

Student A, turn to page 90.
Student B, turn to page 102.

3 **Practice with a partner using the conversation map in exercise 2. Use your own ideas for company, names, number, and message. Use the chart to make notes.**

Company:

Name:

Number:

Message:

1 **Look at the charts. They show phrases you can use to make appointments.**

When are you free? When is good for you? What time is good for you?	
Are you free	(on Monday)? (at two o'clock)? (on the 25th)?
How about	(Monday)? (five o'clock)?

I'm free	(on Tuesday). (at 11:30).
Sorry,	I'm busy then.
Yes,	I'm free then.
That's fine. Five o'clock is fine.	

2 🎧 **1.43 Listen to these conversations. Where and when will they meet? Check your answers with a partner.**

Conversation 1

Day:

Time:

Place:

Conversation 2

Day:

Time:

Place:

Conversation 3

Day:

Time:

Place:

3 **Practice with a partner using your own names. Follow this conversation map.**

Caller:

"Ring, ring."

Give your name. Ask how he / she is.

Reply. Say you are calling to ask if he / she is free for a meeting.

Ask if he / she is free on (day).

Say that is fine. Ask if he / she is free at (time).

Confirm day and time.

End the call.

Receiver:

Give your name. Offer to help.

Reply and reflect (*And you?*).

Say you will check your schedule. Ask when is good for him / her.

Say you are busy then. Give another day.

Agree.

Agree.

End the call.

Viewpoints: Using technology to communicate

1 💿 **1.44 Listen to people from three different countries talking about how they communicate. Make notes as you listen.**

Kay West, Project manager, U.S.	**Tran Chung Nguyen,** Assistant sales manager, Vietnam	**Masako Mori,** H.R. officer, Japan
Notes:	Notes:	Notes:
Email:	Email:	Email:
Voicemail:	Voicemail:	Voicemail:
Telephone:	Telephone:	Telephone:
Teleconference:	Teleconference:	Teleconference:
Meetings:	Meetings:	Meetings:

2 Check (✓) the boxes with your own information.

	Use	**Don't use**	**Like**	**Don't like**
Email				
Telephone				
Teleconference				
Face-to-face				
Text messages				
Chat				

3 Talk about your answers in a small group. Try to use some of this vocabulary.

complicated   efficient   formal   inefficient   informal   quick   simple   slow

For example:

A: *Do you use email?*

B: *Yes, I do. / No, I don't. How about you?*

A: *I like email because it's quick. What do you think?*

C: *Me too. I don't like chat because it's informal. How about you?*

Project: Make an appointment

Review

How much do you remember about other companies advertisements? In a group, try to describe some of the advertisements and see if you can remember the key points.

it was really... *energy-efficient*

it was a bit... *fast* *compact*

it wasn't very... *cheap* *light*

Begin like this: *Your advertisement said your jackets are very warm. And they're now 10% off. Is that right?*

Activity

1 Fill out next week's schedule for your employee. Put in three or four activities (e.g., meeting, vacation, business trip) but leave some room to schedule appointments.

	MONDAY	TUESDAY	WEDNESDAY	THURSDAY	FRIDAY
9:00		Visit			
10:00		Customer			
11:00				Meeting	
12:00	Lunch			Lunch	
1:00					
2:00					
3:00					
4:00					
5:00					
6:00			Teleconference		

2 Call a partner to make an appointment. Say why you want to meet. Then write down on the schedule the person's name and reason for the meeting. Change partners and make another appointment. Make at least six appointments.

1   **Describe the picture. Where are they? What are they saying?**

2   🔊 **1.45 Listen to the conversation. Circle the correct answer.**

   a   Andy is at *his / someone else's* company.

   b   Andy *knows / doesn't know* where to go.

3   🔊 **1.45 Listen again and complete the conversation. Then practice with a partner. Take turns being the receptionist and Andy.**

Receptionist:	Can I _____ you?
Andy:	Yes. I'm Andy Johnson, and I have a 3:00 appointment with Jack Huang in Marketing.
Receptionist:	OK, Mr. Johnson, you can go _____ up.
Andy:	Thanks. Uh… how do I _____ _____ the Marketing Department?
Receptionist:	Oh, it's on the third floor. When you _____ out of the elevator, turn right and _____ _____ the hall. It's the second door on your left, and it says "Marketing Department" on it. You can't _____ it.
Andy:	Thanks. Oh, and, uh, _____ the elevator?

4   **Now practice the conversation again. Change the information in blue using the information below.**

Andy	10:30 a.m. meeting		Production	
	lunch appointment		Sales	
	2:00 p.m. appointment		Accounting	
Receptionist	seventh	turn right	the first room after the stairs	Production
	second	go straight	the last room on your right	Sales
	fourth	turn left	just after the drinking fountain	Accounting

5 🔊 1.46 **What do you think the receptionist will do next? Check (✓) your guesses. Then listen to see if you are correct.**

a ☐ She will tell Andy where the elevator is.

b ☐ She will draw a map.

c ☐ She will call Mr. Huang in Marketing.

d ☐ She will take Andy to the third floor.

Prepositions of place

across from
between
in the corner
next to / on the right
behind
in front of
next to / on the left
under

1 **Where is the desk? Label each picture with words and phrases from the box.**

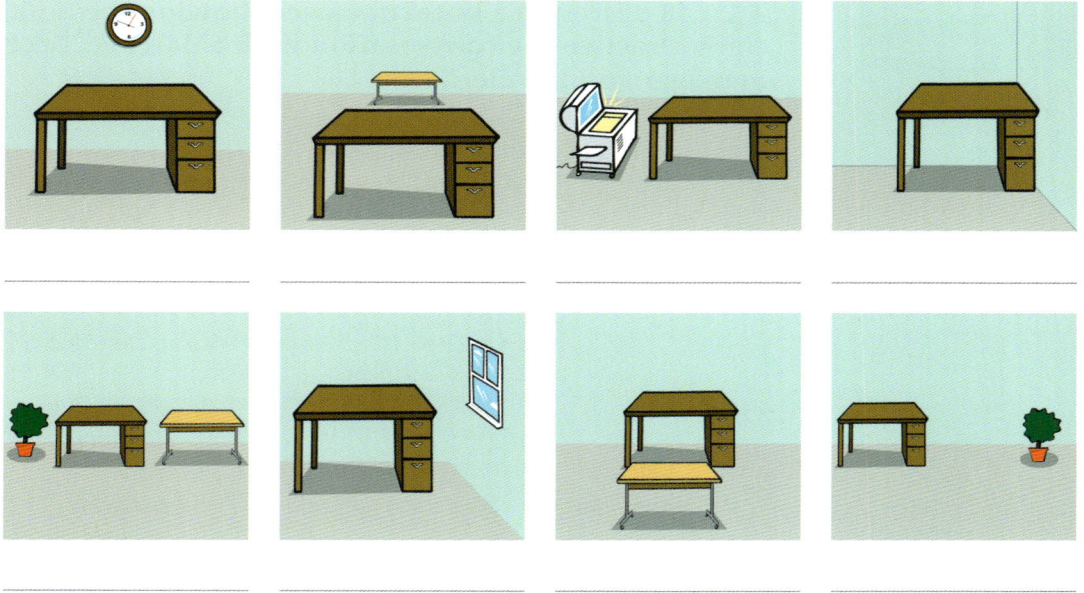

2 🔊 1.47 **Listen to two people talking about an office. Label the desks that belong to these people. Write the correct letter on the desk.**

a the boss   **b** the secretary   **c** Ken   **d** Sophie

Talk business

Student A, turn to page 91.

Student B, turn to page 103.

3 **Look at the office on page 51. Practice with a partner asking and answering questions about the picture.**

For example: **A:** *Excuse me. Where's the fax machine?*

B: *Oh, it's over there, next to Sophie's desk, on the right.*

Now ask and answer questions about these things:

a coffee maker   **b** plant   **c** drinking fountain   **d** exit

Giving a tour

1 🔊 **1.48** **Listen to a hotel manager showing the hotel to a new front desk clerk. Practice the conversation with a partner. Take turns being the manager and the clerk.**

Manager:	Come with me, please. OK, this is the lobby, of course. There's an ATM machine in the corner there. Oh, and a public phone, next to the ATM machine. Any questions?
Clerk:	Yes, is the lobby open 24 hours?
Manager:	Yes, it is. Now, let's go to the elevators. They're next to the stairs. This elevator on the left goes only to the rooms. It doesn't stop on the second, third, or fourth floors. And this one here, this one stops on every floor. We'll go first to the second floor – that's the dining room and the lounge – and then to the third floor, the business center. Um, any questions so far?
Clerk:	What's on the fourth floor?
Manager:	The swimming pool and the fitness center. OK, come with me.

2 **Look at the chart. It shows directions and questions you can use when you talk to groups of people.**

Directions	Questions
Come with me, please. Follow me.	Any questions? Is that clear? Are you with me so far?
Listen carefully. Watch closely.	Can everyone hear me? Can everyone see?
Let's go now. Let's stop here.	Is everyone with me?

3 🎧 1.49 **Listen to these group tours. Check (✓) the question that you hear. Then write the response.**

a ☐ Are you with me so far?   *No, Sandy's at the drinking fountain.*
   ☐ Is everyone with me?

b ☐ Can everyone see?   _____
   ☐ Any questions?

c ☐ OK? Is that clear?   _____
   ☐ OK? Can you hear?

d ☐ Is everyone here?   _____
   ☐ Can everyone hear me?

4 **Work in groups of 3–5. One of you is the HR manager of a factory. The others are new employees. Take turns being the manager and give the new employees a tour. Use the map below. Start at the "X."**

Begin like this:

OK, follow me, please. Let's go straight down this path. On the left is the research laboratory. …

Viewpoints: Workplace facilities

1   Read what these people say about their workplaces.

Rodrigo de Santos,
Marketing executive, Brazil

I work for a small marketing company. At the office, we only have a small cafeteria and some **vending machines**. But my company gives us discounts at many local businesses, including restaurants, stores, health **clinics**, hotels, and a health club.

Young-kwang Oh,
Factory worker, Korea

I work in a factory. Because we often work overtime, and because there are a lot of different **shifts**, workers don't always have time to go shopping during the week. So we have a small **convenience store** on site, and also an ATM, a **pharmacy**, a hair salon, and a **laundry** service.

Lise Martin,
Clerk, Canada

I work for an **insurance** company. Ten years ago, we had on-site daycare. But the company found out that working parents preferred a **flexible** schedule. Now we have **facilities** like a cafeteria, a gym, and a locker room. There's also a **yoga** class that meets twice a week during the lunch hour.

2   Imagine you are working at a medium-sized company five years from now. How important would these facilities be to you? Check (✓) the appropriate column.

	very important / necessary	not necessary, but attractive	not interesting or useful to me
on-site daycare			
a gym			
a cafeteria			
a convenience store			
a bank or an ATM			
a pharmacy			
a hair salon			
showers			
a travel agency			

3   Now talk about your answers in a small group, and discuss these questions.

a   What other facilities would you like your company to have?

b   Do you think your answers would be different 10 or 15 years from now?

Project: Give a company tour

Review

Look back at the appointments you made in Unit 7, page 49. Choose two appointments to cancel, and one appointment to reschedule.

Cancel an appointment like this:

A: Hi, (*name*). This is (*your name*). Listen, I have to cancel our (*meeting*) on (*Thursday*) at (*3:00*). Something's come up. I'm really sorry. I'll call or email you next week about rescheduling.

B: That's OK, I understand. I look forward to hearing from you next week.

Reschedule an appointment like this:

A: Hi, (*name*). This is (*your name*). Listen, something's come up. I need to reschedule our (*meeting*) on (*Thursday*) at (*3:00*). Are you free on (*Friday*) at (*10:00*)?

B: *Yes, that's fine. / Sorry, I'm busy then. How about … .*

Cross out your canceled appointments. Write down your rescheduled appointment.

Activity

1 What facilities does your company have? Make a list here.

2 Now draw a map of your company or a part of your company. Include some of the facilities you listed in exercise 1. Use a separate sheet of paper.

3 Work in a small group. Using your map, give your classmates a tour of your company. Use the language you learned for talking to groups of people. Then tour their companies!

Review: Units 5–8

1 Be polite

Change the conversation to make it more polite. Then practice with a partner.

Receptionist: BL Chemicals.

Kevin: I want Jon Philpott.

Receptionist: What's your name?

Kevin: Kevin Aston, Ashwell Transportation.

Receptionist: Can't hear. Say it louder.

Kevin: Kevin Aston. Ashwell Transportation.

Receptionist: Spell your family name.

Kevin: A-S-T-O-N.

Receptionist: Wait.

_____

_____

_____

_____

_____

_____

2 Controlling language

What can you say if …

someone speaks too quietly?

_____

someone speaks too quickly?

_____

you want someone to repeat something?

_____

you want someone to spell something?

_____

3 Conversation map

Use this map to have a telephone conversation with a partner.

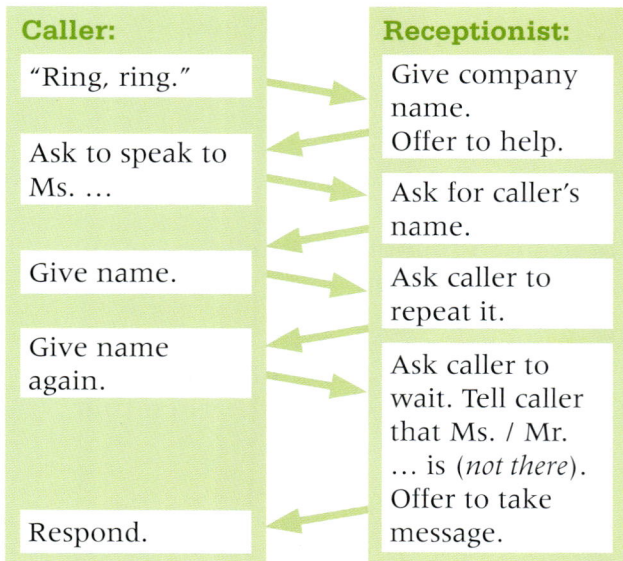

Caller:	Receptionist:
"Ring, ring."	Give company name. Offer to help.
Ask to speak to Ms. …	Ask for caller's name.
Give name.	Ask caller to repeat it.
Give name again.	Ask caller to wait. Tell caller that Ms. / Mr. … is (*not there*). Offer to take message.
Respond.	

4 Word square

Hidden in the square are 12 adjectives to describe products. How many words can you find in five minutes? (Look in these directions: ↓→)

g	e	o	i	s	t	e	n	d	f	r	a
a	w	r	e	l	i	a	b	l	e	q	c
i	d	a	s	e	p	s	l	i	t	u	o
b	s	t	m	e	r	y	x	g	t	f	m
t	t	x	a	y	r	r	n	h	i	s	p
e	r	n	l	i	w	s	j	t	u	t	a
a	o	d	l	e	t	t	i	k	v	i	c
a	n	u	e	f	f	i	c	i	e	n	t
r	g	o	w	f	t	s	e	v	l	o	d
t	z	k	s	s	b	u	f	l	a	s	p
e	h	e	a	v	y	r	a	v	i	c	e
n	o	f	f	l	i	k	s	c	o	h	e
m	a	t	t	r	a	c	t	i	v	e	g
u	r	d	l	u	s	h	a	n	e	a	t
d	e	l	i	c	i	o	u	s	i	p	s

5 What's the difference?

Use the adjectives in exercise 4 to compare the products. Which do you like better? Why?

6 to or about?

Complete the expressions with *to* or *about*. Then read them out loud with a partner.

I'm calling…

a _____ confirm my reservation.
b _____ my visit tomorrow.
c _____ change our meeting time.
d _____ your order #43256.
e _____ our appointment this afternoon.
f _____ ask if we can meet.
g _____ request some information.
h _____ lunch today.

7 Are you free on Monday?

Practice with a partner. Use this conversation map and use your own names.

Caller:	Receiver:
"Ring, ring."	Give your name.
Give your name. Ask how he / she is.	
	Reply.
Reply. Say you are calling to ask if he / she is free for a meeting.	Ask him / her to speak louder.
Repeat (louder).	

8 Where's the bank?

Add these places to the map:

bank   movie theater   drugstore   post office
Then take turns giving a tour to other people.

Step 1 → Step 2 ⇄ Step 3 → Step 4

Listen and practice

1 **Describe the pictures. What is happening? What are they doing?**

2 🔊 **1.50 Sarah is describing Comet's design process to Hari and May. Listen and write T for true or F for false next to each sentence.**

  a   The first step is planning the design. _____

  b   The final step is to launch the web page. _____

3 🔊 **1.50 Listen again and complete the conversation. Then practice with two partners. Take turns being Hari, May, and Sarah.**

Sarah: _____ _____ talk to the customers or users of the web page. This is the most important step, to find out what the customer needs. _____ _____ , we plan the basic design of the web page. _____ _____ layout of text, graphics, and languages.

Hari: I see. And what do you do next?

Sarah: The _____ _____ is we pilot the web page and get feedback from customers.

May: Yes, customer feedback is very important.

Sarah: _____we get feedback we revise the design and make any changes or improvements. _____ _____ launch the new web page. Are there any questions?

4 🔊 **1.51 What questions do you think Hari and May will ask?**
Check (✓) your guesses. Then listen to see if you are correct.

a ☐ How long does the process take?
b ☐ What color is the web page?
c ☐ Who are the customers?
d ☐ How much does it cost?

Describing a process

sequencing

1 Look at the chart. It shows ways you can describe the steps in a process.

First Second Third Fourth ………	After (that)… Before… Next… Then… At the same time… Finally…
The (first) step is…	

2 Look at these flow charts. Practice with a partner. Take turns describing the processes.

Begin like this: *There are ___ steps in this process. First you…*

a) A cup of tea – English style

Heat the water. → Put a tea bag in the cup. → Pour boiling water into the cup. → Wait for 3–4 minutes. → Take out the tea bag. → Add milk or a slice of lemon.

b) A mango smoothie

Peel and chop the fruit. → Add the fruit to the blender. → Add ice cubes and some yogurt. → Blend for about 1 minute. → Pour the smoothie into glasses.

1 a Write these sentences under the illustrations.

We send an invoice.	We enter the data.
We order the product from the factory.	We check the inventory.
We arrange delivery.	We receive the order.

b 🔊 1.52 Then listen and check your answers.

2 With a partner, use the sentences in exercise 1 to order the steps in the flow chart.

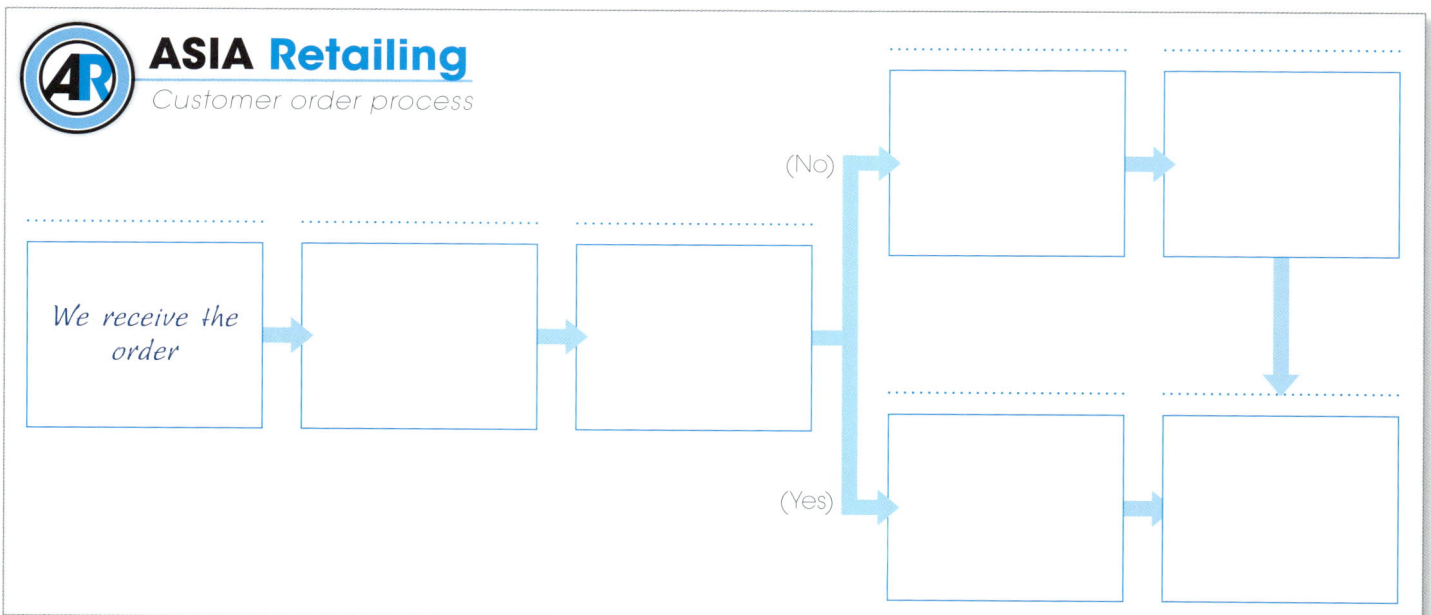

ASIA **Retailing**
Customer order process

We receive the order

(No)

(Yes)

3 🔊 **1.52 Listen again. Next to each step write down the sequencing language May uses.**

4 Now describe the process to a partner. You can use the same language as May or you can change some of the language.

Conversation strategy review

checking and confirming

1 Look at the charts. They show ways you can check and confirm understanding.

Is that clear (so far)?	Yes, that's clear.
Are you with me (so far)?	I understand / I'm with you. OK.
OK?	Let me confirm that, … Let me repeat that, …

2 Choose one of the following and describe it to a partner. Remember to check and confirm the information.

How to use a cell phone camera
How to make a photocopy
How to boil an egg
How to shampoo and condition your hair
How to brush your teeth
(your idea)

Describing a process

recruiting

Work in a group. Using these steps, describe a recruiting process. Choose one option from Steps 1, 2, and 3.

Begin like this: *There are four steps in our recruiting process. First we …*

STEP 1	Advertise online	Visit universities	Advertise in newspapers
STEP 2	Receive résumés by mail	Receive résumés online	
STEP 3	Give one-on-one interviews	Give group interviews	Give a written test
STEP 4	Choose the best employee!		

👥 Talk business

Student A, turn to page 92.
Student B, turn to page 104.

Viewpoints: Looking for a job

1 🔘 **1.53** Listen to people from three countries talking about how they looked for a job. Match the person with what they say.

| It takes about a year! | I talked to my professor and he **recommended** an **internship**. | I went to 15 or 20 interviews. |

a Junko Saito,
Designer, Japan

b Jean Durand,
Engineer, France

c Susan Russell,
Trainee manager, U.S.

| I looked on the Internet. | After I **graduated** the company offered me a job. | You can't get experience without a job! |

2 🔘 **1.53** Now listen again and check (✓) what method each person used to look for a job.

	Junko	Jean	Susan
Attended job fair			
Visited university job center			
Friend's advice / recommendation			
Newspaper advertisement			
Professor's advice / recommendation			
Internet / website			

3 How do people in your country look for jobs after college or university? Talk about your answers in a small group.

Project: Design a process

Review

Talk to the people whose tours you took in Unit 8. Thank them for the tour and tell them some things you liked.

For example:

Thank you for the tour of the candy factory. I liked seeing the candy-making machines. The showroom was very interesting. And the free samples were delicious!

Activity

1   In the space below, or on a separate sheet of paper, draw a flow chart for a process in your company. You can use your own idea or you can use one of the suggestions.

• How products are ordered	• How new employees are recruited
• How a new product is developed	• Your own idea: _____

Process: _____

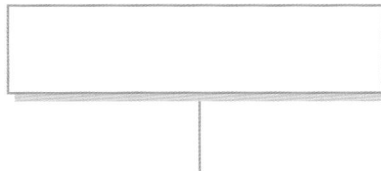

2   Work with a partner. Describe your process and check / confirm understanding. After you have finished, change partners and repeat the exercise.

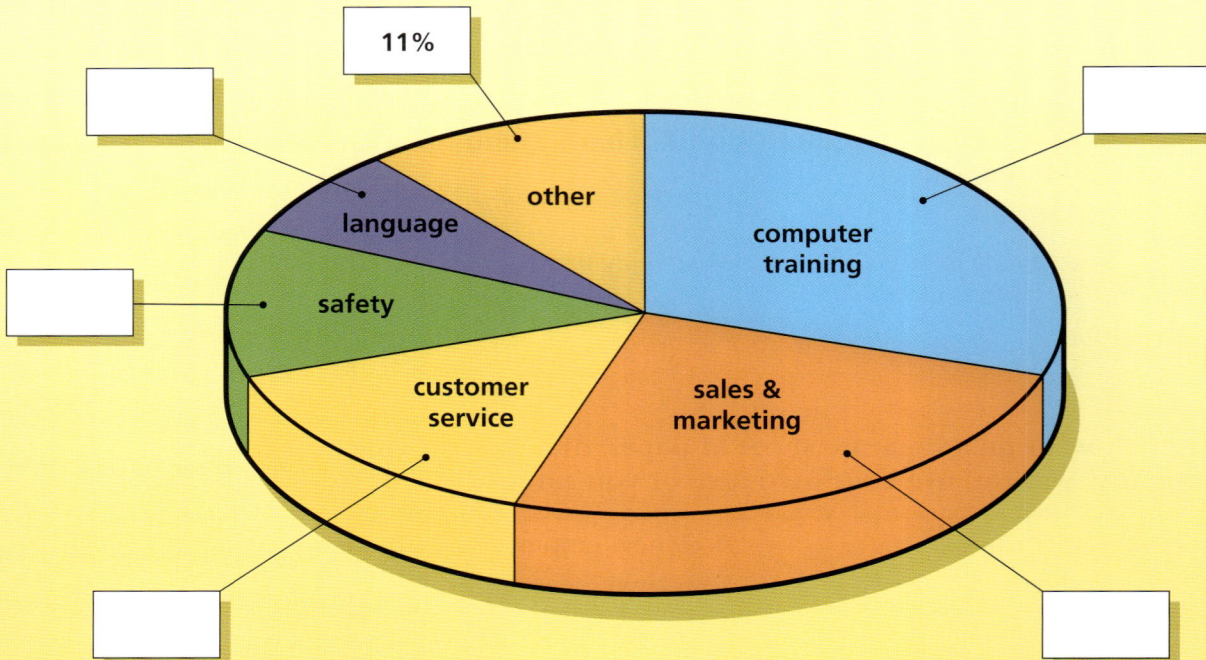

11%

other

language

safety

computer
training

customer
service

sales &
marketing

1 **Look at the pie chart. What does it show?**

2 🔊 **2.01 Listen to Hari's presentation to AR's Marketing Department. What is the presentation about? Circle the correct answer.**

   a How to use the new computer system

   b How to spend money for training

   c Why language training is too expensive

3 🔊 **2.01 Listen again and complete the pie chart with the correct numbers.**

4 **Practice with a partner. Change the information in blue using the information in the pie chart. Take turns explaining the pie chart.**

   They spent 35 percent of the training budget on computers.

5 🔊 **2.02 What do you think Hari will do next? Check (✓) your guesses. Then listen to see if you are correct.**

   a ☐ He will suggest that everyone take a break.

   b ☐ He will talk about next year's training needs.

   c ☐ He will talk about how much money the company has now.

   d ☐ He will check to see if anyone has any questions.

1 Look at the bar graph. What does it show? Why do you think the information is presented in a graph?

exports (in units)

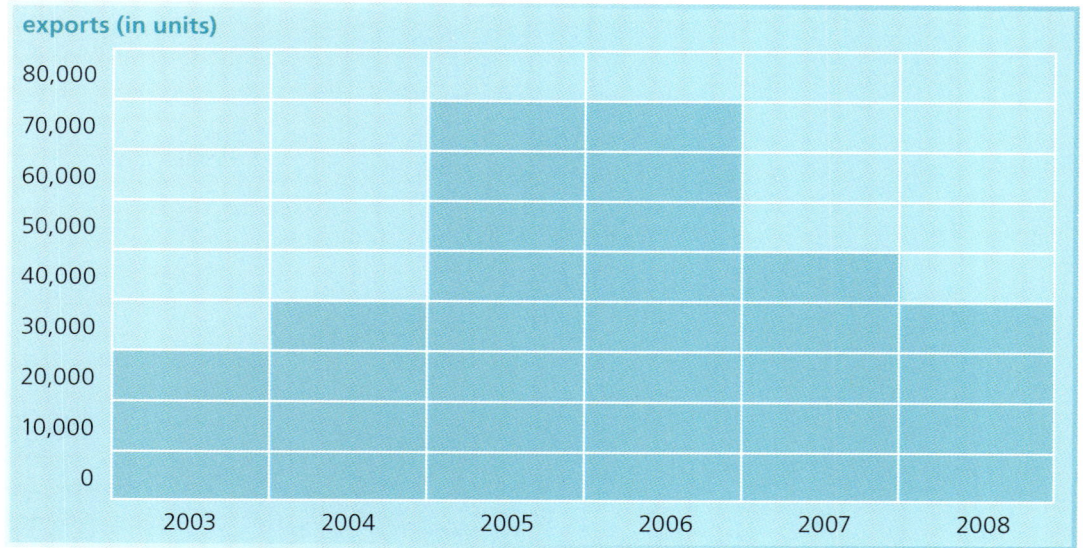

| | 2003 | 2004 | 2005 | 2006 | 2007 | 2008 |

2 Look at the chart. It shows ways you can talk about information in a graph. Look at the bar graph in exercise 1 again, and write the correct year in the chart. Then take turns reading the sentences with a partner.

	… increased	sharply			in		_2005_
		slightly			in		_____
Exports	… decreased	sharply	from	_____	to		_____
		slightly			in		_____
	… stayed about the same		from	_____	to		_____

3 🔊 **2.03** Listen to May giving a presentation about the number of customer complaints her department received last year. Draw in the correct bars on the graph.

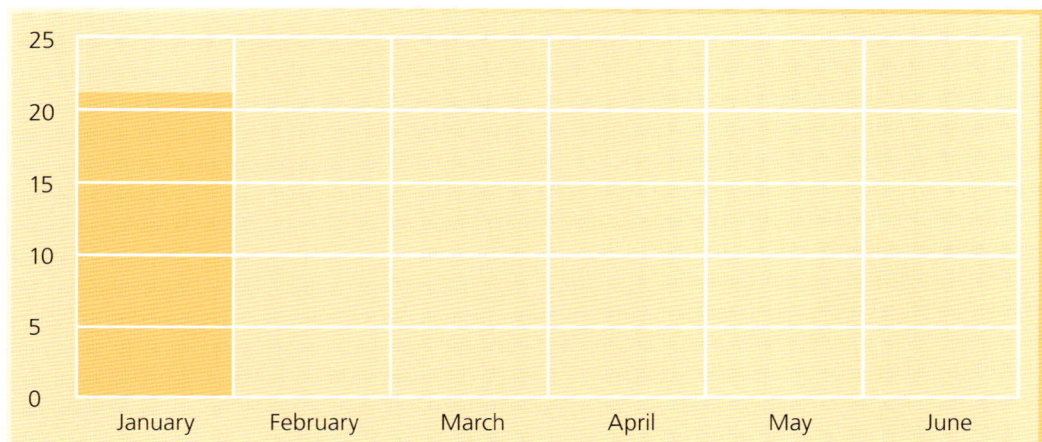

| | January | February | March | April | May | June |

1 Look at these sentences that people use when they give presentations. When do you think people say them? Copy the sentences into the correct place in the chart.

OK, can everybody see?

Is everybody here?

Is everybody with me so far?

We're finished for today.

Let's get started.

Let's take a five-minute break.

As you can see here, …

That's all for now.

Thanks for listening
Are there any questions?

At the beginning	In the middle	At the end

2 2.04 Listen to the presentations. Check (✓) the sentences you hear.

a ☐ Let's get started.
☐ We'll begin at 10:00.

c ☐ Are there any questions so far?
☐ Is everybody with me so far?

b ☐ As you can see here, …
☐ Can everybody see?

d ☐ That's all for today.
☐ I think we're finished.

Talk business

Student A, turn to page 93.
Student B, turn to page 105.

1 🔊 **2.05** **After a presentation, we often ask our audience if there are any questions. But what happens if you don't know the answer? Listen to these ways you can respond. Then practice with a partner.**

a
> A: Excuse me, how much will the new computers cost?
> B: **I'm sorry, I'm not really sure. I'll check on that and get back to you.**
> A: Thanks, I'd appreciate that.

b
> A: When is the next training session?
> B: **I'm sorry, I don't know. I'll check with** Pam **and let you know**.
> A: OK, thanks.

c
> A: Is this information available in a document?
> B: **Actually, I'm not sure. Let me check on that for you.**
> A: Oh, that's OK, it's not important.

2 **Work with a partner. Take turns asking the questions and responding. Use the conversations in exercise 1 as models.**

a What's the population of Russia?
b Who is the prime minister of Australia?
c How much does an average apartment in Paris cost?
d When was the Internet invented?
e How many people speak Mandarin?
f What are the official languages of Sri Lanka?
g What is the CEO's salary?
h How many employees are there in Taiwan?

Viewpoints: Presentations

1 Read what these people say about giving and attending presentations. Which kinds of presentations have you given or attended?

Mei-ling Chen,
Project manager, Singapore

We have customers from many different companies, so our presentations are in English. We use a lot of charts and graphs to make sure everyone understands the information. Some of our presentations are pretty long, so we sometimes take a tea break in the middle.

Tasha Green,
Administrative clerk, U.S.

These days, most people use some kind of presentation software like PowerPoint. Sometimes the presentations look really good, but I don't like it when people just read their **slides** to you. That's boring.

Viktor Brodsky,
C.E.O, Ukraine

I prefer to just talk during my presentations. I don't want to worry about using equipment and graphs and charts. If you depend on equipment and it doesn't work, then what happens to your presentation?

2 Which kinds of presentations do you like? Put a check (✓) on the bar closest to your opinion. Then talk about your opinions in a group. (If you haven't attended or given any presentations, answer about a school class.)

no opinion; either is fine

I like long presentations.						I like short presentations.
It's OK if I don't know the topic in advance.						I want to know the topic in advance.
Eating and drinking is distracting.						I like to drink coffee or tea, or have a snack.
Only the presenter should talk.						Everyone should give their opinions.
The atmosphere should be formal. I don't like a lot of joking around.						I like an informal atmosphere. It's OK if the presenter tells some jokes.
People should ask questions at the end of the presentation.						People should ask questions whenever they think of them.
I like just listening during a presentation – no visual aids.						I prefer some kind of visual aid, like PowerPoint or a graph or chart.

Project: Give a presentation

Review

Work with the partner who described a process to you in Unit 9, page 63.
How much do you remember? Tell your partner.

For example: **A:** *You described how your sportswear is made.*

             B: *Yes, that's right!*

             A: *First, you designed the sportswear. Next, you sold it in your stores.*

             B: *Actually, next, we made it in our factories.*

Activity

1 Choose some information about your company to present in a
graph or chart. Check (✓) your topic:

- [ ] sales figures from one year
- [ ] sales figures from more than one year
- [ ] types of products your company has
- [ ] the budget for one department
- [ ] the number of imports or exports over a period of several months or years
- [ ] the number of employees who work in each department in your company
- [ ] the number or type of customer complaints
- [ ] your idea: _____

2 Now draw a pie chart or bar graph to present your information.

3 Work in groups or with the whole class. Take turns giving your presentation.
Don't forget to start and end your presentation with the language on page 66,
and to check understanding during your presentation. After you listen
to your classmates' presentations, ask them questions!

11 | I'm leaving tomorrow

Now

Tonight

Tomorrow

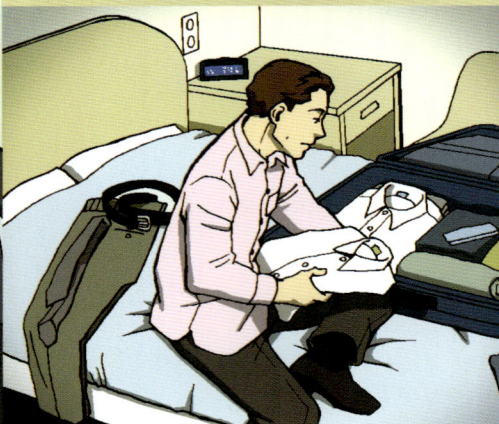

1   Describe the pictures. What is happening?

_____

2   🔘 **2.06**   **Hari and Andy are meeting. Listen to the conversation. Write T for true or F for false next to each sentence.**

   a   Hari will send the contract by the 5th. _____

   b   Andy is leaving this weekend. _____

_____

3   🔘 **2.06**   **Listen again and complete the conversation. Then practice with a partner. Take turns being Hari and Andy.**

Hari: OK, let me confirm our next steps. _____ _____ _____ send us a cost estimate by the end of this week. Is that right?

Andy: That's right, and _____ _____ prepare the contract?

Hari: Yes, we'll send it to you by the 15th. Is that OK?

Andy: That's great. _____ _____ working on this right away.

Hari: Great! _____ _____ _____ back this weekend?

Andy: Yes, I'm leaving tomorrow morning.

Hari: What _____ _____ _____ this evening?

Andy: Nothing special. I'm going to pack my suitcases.

_____

4   **Now practice the conversation again. Change the information in blue using the information below.**

deliver the parts this afternoon	prepare the invoice	by Friday
arrange a meeting by the 12th	make the agenda	by tomorrow
meet the customer tomorrow	check the address	today
finish the report by five o'clock	send the data	by lunchtime

5 🔊 2.07 **What do you think Hari will say next? Check (✓) your guesses. Then listen to see if you are correct.**

a ☐ Where is your hotel?   **c** ☐ How many suitcases do you have?

b ☐ Have a good flight!   **d** ☐ Would you like to have dinner?

Talking about future plans

1 **Look at the chart. It shows ways you can talk about future plans.**

Form	Example	Meaning
will	I will finish the report tomorrow	intention, promise
	Don't worry, I'll help you.	just decided
be going to	We're going to meet him today.	already planned
verb + -ing	I'm leaving tomorrow.	already planned (usually near future)

2 🔊 2.08 **Listen to these five conversations. Match the conversation with the picture. Number the pictures in order 1–5.**

3 🔊 2.08 **Now listen again and complete these sentences from the conversations. Check your answers with a partner.**

a Don't worry, _____*I'll help*_____ you find it.   (help)

b 6:30. _____ a taxi to the airport.   (take)

c My friends _____ at the airport.   (meet)

d I'm too tired. _____ tomorrow.   (go shopping)

e Tomorrow _____ a barbecue.   (have)

f On Sunday _____ my apartment.   (clean up)

g I'm not sure. Perhaps _____ a movie.   (watch)

h Just a minute, _____ the help desk.   (call)

4 Look at the chart. It shows ways you can ask about future plans.

What are you going to do What are you doing	tomorrow? next week? tonight? next Sunday?

With a partner, ask about future plans. Then change partners and repeat the exercise.

5 Here are some other verbs you can use to talk about future plans. With a different partner, talk about your plans for three, five, and ten years from now.

For example:
Five years from now I hope to work in Europe.

| Three years from now, | I | plan to
am planning to | visit London.
buy a house. |
| | | hope to
am hoping to | be the sales manager. |

6 2.09 Listen and draw lines to connect the company with their plans. Describe the plans. Then check your answers with a partner.

a	Marco Supermarkets	increase sales in Asia	next year
b	Pusan Pipe Manufacturing	open four more stores	this year
c	Timson Watches	hire more staff	in the next two years
d	Aztec Coffee	build a new plant	three years from now

Talk business

Student A, turn to page 94.

Student B, turn to page 106.

1 Look at the chart. It shows adverbs you can use to show how certain we are about something.

definitely	definitely not	stronger
probably	probably not	↓
perhaps / maybe	perhaps not / maybe not	weaker

2 In groups of three, ask and answer these questions.

For example: **A:** *Do you think it'll rain tomorrow?*
B: *Maybe. How about you?*
A: *Probably not. What do you think?*
C: *Definitely not.*

1 Do you think it'll rain next weekend?
2 Do you think you'll travel overseas next year?
3 Do you think you'll work for a big company?

3 Look at these sentences; they show the position of the adverb. Practice saying them with a partner.

I'll **definitely** send the invoice today.	I **definitely** won't finish the report today.
We're **probably** going to visit Malaysia next week.	We're **probably** not going to the meeting next week.

Perhaps I'll take a day off tomorrow.
Maybe I'll visit New York next year.
Do you think you'll visit the factory next week? I **probably** will.

4 How sure are you about these statements? Talk about your answers in a group.

a I'll work overseas.

b I'll run a marathon next year.

c In five years I'll be on TV.

d I'll use English in my job.

Viewpoints: Talking about the future

1 💿 **2.10** Listen to people from three different countries talking about their futures. Write down the degree of certainty next to their plans.

Ji-young Kim,
Office worker, Korea

I'll _definitely_ stay with this company.
I'll _____ go to America to study.
_____ I will be a manager.
I'll _____ get married sometime.
I _____ want to **continue** working after I get married.

Amnuay Chaichan,
Assistant sales manager, Thailand

THAI RESTAU

I'll _____ travel around Europe.
I _____ want to take my family with me.

Julie Howe,
Construction worker, Canada

_____ I'll work in the U.S. for a few years.
I _____ want to come back to Canada.

2 In groups of three, pretend you are one of the people in exercise 1. Tell the others about your future plans.

3 Do you know what you want to do in the future? What are some of your future hopes, plans, and dreams? Make some notes in the chart below. Talk about your future plans in a small group.

Time Frame	Event / Action

Project: Describe future plans

Review

Draw a simple line or bar graph on a separate sheet of paper to show sales for your company for the past three years. In a group or with a partner, describe the graph. Begin like this:

Let's get started. This graph shows our sales plan for the past three years. As you can see here, …

Can everybody see?

Are there any questions so far?

…increased slightly…

Thanks for listening.

…stayed about the same…

Activity

1 **How will your company change over the next three, five, or ten years? Are you going to expand your business? Are you planning to open overseas offices? Are you going to hire more people? What will happen to your products?**

What are your plans for your company? Make some notes here:

…open three new stores…

Time frame	Event / Action

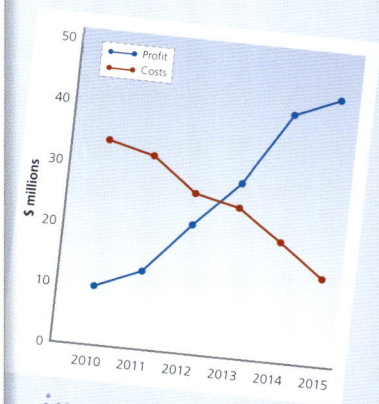

…increase profit…

2 **Talk about your plans in groups. Begin like this:**

Thanks for coming today. I'm going to talk about our future plans. First …

Listen and practice

1 Describe the picture. On a separate sheet of paper, write 3–5 questions about the picture, such as *How many women are there? What's Andy holding?* Then work with a partner. With your books closed, see if you can answer each other's questions!

2 💿 **2.11 Listen to the staff of Asia Retailing entertaining guests from Comet Technologies. Check (✓) the foods and drinks they mention.**

☐ chicken   ☐ coffee   ☐ salad
☐ vegetables   ☐ shrimp   ☐ tea

3 💿 **2.11 Listen again and complete the conversation. Then practice with a partner. Take turns being May and Sarah.**

May: _____ you _____ to try some dim sum?

Sarah: Yes, thank you, they _____ delicious. Um, what's _____ them?

May: These ones have _____ , and these ones have _____ .

Sarah: And, uh, _____ do I eat them?

May: Oh, it's _____ . You _____ one _____ with your chopsticks… like this… and dip it into the sauce.

4 Now practice the conversation again. Change the information in **blue** using the information below.

tacos	beef / beans and cheese	hand	just eat it
samosas	potatoes / meat	fork	put it on your plate
sushi	cucumber / fish	chopsticks	dip it in soy sauce

5 2.12 **What do you think May will do next? Check (✓) your guesses. Then listen to see if you are correct.**

a ☐ She will offer Sarah something to drink.

b ☐ She will ask Sarah if she likes the dim sum.

c ☐ She will tell Sarah how to make dim sum.

d ☐ She will ask Sarah to pass her some food.

Offering and accepting or refusing food

1 **Look at the charts. They show ways you can offer food, and accept or refuse food. Practice with a partner. Take turns reading the questions and answers.**

Questions:	
Would you like to try*	a taco?
Would you like	a cup of coffee? some potato chips? some (more) cake?

*(**Note:** Use *to try* if your guest has not had the food before.)

Answers:		
Yes, please.	It looks They smell That sounds	delicious. wonderful. good.
No, thank you.	I just had one / some. I can't eat any more!	
	I'm	a vegetarian. allergic. on a diet.

2 2.13 **Listen to these conversations. Check (✓) the question that you hear. Then write the response.**

a ☐ Would you like some …? _____
   ☐ Would you like to try some …?

b ☐ Would you like some more …? _____
   ☐ Would you like to try some …?

c ☐ Would you like a …? _____
   ☐ Would you like some …?

d ☐ Would you like some …? _____
   ☐ Would you like some more …?

3 **Practice with a partner. Take turns offering these foods and drinks and accepting or refusing them. Use the information below and your own ideas.**

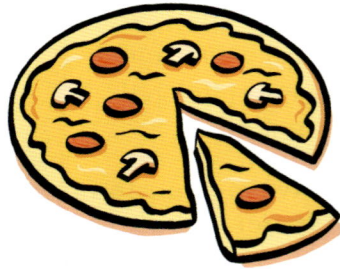

a some pizza

c some chicken curry

Talk business

Student A, turn to page 95.

Student B, turn to page 107.

b a brownie

d an apple

Giving and receiving compliments

1 🔘 2.14 **Listen to the conversations.**

Conversation 1

Guest: This fish is delicious!

Host: No, it isn't. It's too salty and dry.

Guest: Oh. Well, it tastes good to me …

Conversation 2

Guest: This curry is delicious!

Host: Oh, thank you. My daughter made it with me. I hope it's not too spicy.

Guest: No, not at all. What's in it?

Host: Well, chicken, fresh vegetables, and my own spices. Would you like the recipe?

Guest: Yes, thank you. That's very kind of you.

2 **Discuss these questions with a partner.**

a In which conversation does the guest feel uncomfortable? Why? Practice the successful conversation.

b In English, it is common to give compliments. If you receive a compliment, it is polite to accept it (*Thank you*) and then say one or two more sentences about the item that is being complimented (*My daughter made it with me. I hope it's not too spicy.*). What is the custom in your culture?

(**Note:** Do not give compliments on a person's personal appearance. You might hurt someone's feelings, or give the wrong impression. Women can compliment other women on their clothing or accessories, but men should not give these kinds of compliments to women.)

3 Practice with a partner. Take turns giving and accepting compliments. Use the information below and then your own ideas. Use a polite tone of voice!

a garden is lovely / wife planted the roses

c coffee is delicious / from Guatemala

b town is beautiful / many old buildings

d son is very smart / only two years old

Thanking and responding to thanks

1 Look at the chart. Then practice with a partner. Take turns thanking and responding.

Thank you for	lunch. the flowers.	You're welcome. I'm glad you liked it / them. Oh, don't mention it. Oh, not at all.
	inviting me. sending me the report.	

2 Work in a group. Take turns thanking every group member for something. Try to respond to your classmates' thanks in a different way each time.

Thank you for being my partner.   You're welcome.

Thank you for making me laugh.   Oh, don't mention it.

Viewpoints: Food and business entertaining

1 Read what these people from around the world say about food. Which culture is most similar to yours?

Rajiv Das,
Business man, India

Business lunches are more common than business dinners. If you are served **traditional** Indian food, remember to eat only with the right hand – even if you are **left-handed**! In addition, do not use your hands to take food from a **communal** dish. Muslims do not eat pork, and Hindus do not eat beef, so vegetarian dishes are common.

Dmitri Petrov,
Product planner, Russia

Russians **appreciate** a good supply of different snacks and drinks at business meetings. Both the food and the serving dishes (plates, cups, and so on) should be of good quality. If you are invited to a Russian's home, you will be offered a lot of food! It is polite to bring a gift if you are the guest.

Lucia Rossi,
C.E.O., Argentina

Business **entertaining** is very common. We usually invite guests to dinner at a restaurant, not a private home. We don't talk about business over dinner, though – it's a time to get to know one another on a **social** level. Meat, especially local beef, is a popular dish. Dinners start at around 10:00 p.m.

2 What kind of foods do you like to eat on these occasions? Make a quick list.

for breakfast
_____
_____

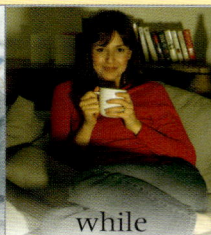
while watching TV
_____
_____

for dessert
_____
_____

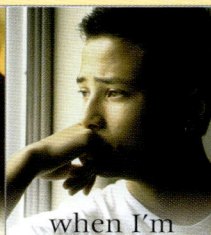
when I'm unhappy
_____
_____

at a birthday party
_____
_____

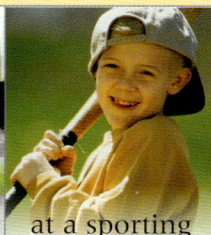
at a sporting event
_____
_____

3 Compare your answers in a group. How would you explain any foods that an international visitor would not know? Tell the group. Do you all enjoy the same kinds of food?

Project: A business party

Review

Work with a partner who listened to your presentation from Unit 11. How much does he or she remember? Test your partner. Say three sentences about your company's future plans, two true and one false. Your partner then guesses which sentence is false.

For example: **A:** *My company is going to expand next year.*

B: *That's true.*

A: *Correct. My company is hoping to build a factory in China in the next three years.*

B: *That's false.*

A: *Actually, that's true.*

Activity

1 **Plan a business party. Your employee will be the host. Invite some of your classmates' employees.**

What is the reason for the party? _____

Who will you invite? _____

What will you serve? Choose your food and drinks:

snacks	food	drinks

2 **Now role-play your party in a group or with the whole class. Use this conversation map.**

Host:

Offer some food or drink.

If the guest refuses, offer something else until the guest accepts.

Accept the compliment and give more information.

Accept the thanks.

Say good-bye.

Guest:

Accept
or
Refuse (say why).

Compliment the food or drink.

Thank the host.

Say goodbye.

Review: Units 9–12

1 Where's it from?

Match the food to the country. Then use the conversation map to offer and accept.

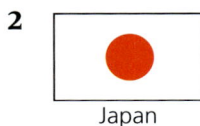

1 England

2 Japan

3 Italy

4 America

5 China

a sushi

b hamburger

c dim sum

d roast beef

e pasta

Host:		Guest:
Offer some food.	→	Accept. Ask where it's from.
Respond.	←	Compliment the food.
Accept the compliment.	←	

3 What's the next step?

2.15 Listen and complete the steps in the process. Then describe the process to a partner.

a c _ _ _ _ _ _ _ _ o _ _ _ _ _

b m _ _ _ _ _ _ t _ _ _ _ g

c t _ _ _ _ n _

d s _ _ _ _ _ _ _ g

2 Finish the graph!

Complete the graph and add a title. Describe the graph to a partner.

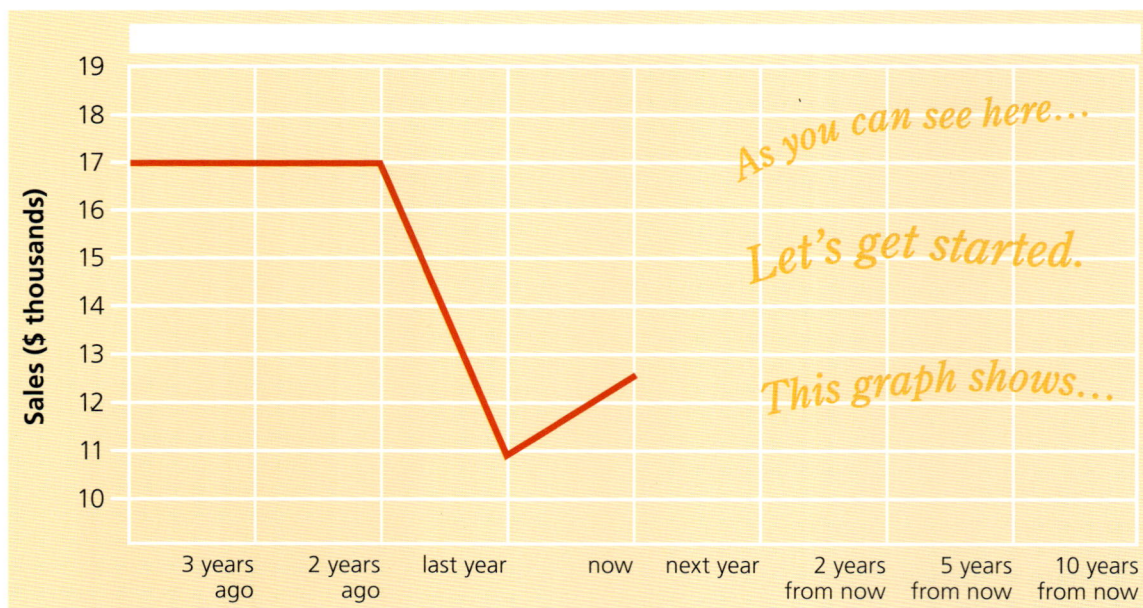

As you can see here…

Let's get started.

This graph shows…

Sales ($ thousands)

19
18
17
16
15
14
13
12
11
10

3 years ago · 2 years ago · last year · now · next year · 2 years from now · 5 years from now · 10 years from now

4 Great job!

Match the compliment with the response. Then practice with a partner.

a   I enjoyed your presentation!   Thank you. We moved here last month.
b   I like your bag!   Thank you! They're chocolate chip. My daughter made them.
c   These are nice offices!   Thank you. It was a present from my mother.
d   These are delicious!   Thank you! It took me a long time to make the slides.

5 Q&A

With a partner ask and answer questions about the graph.
Then student A gives an answer, and student B makes the question.

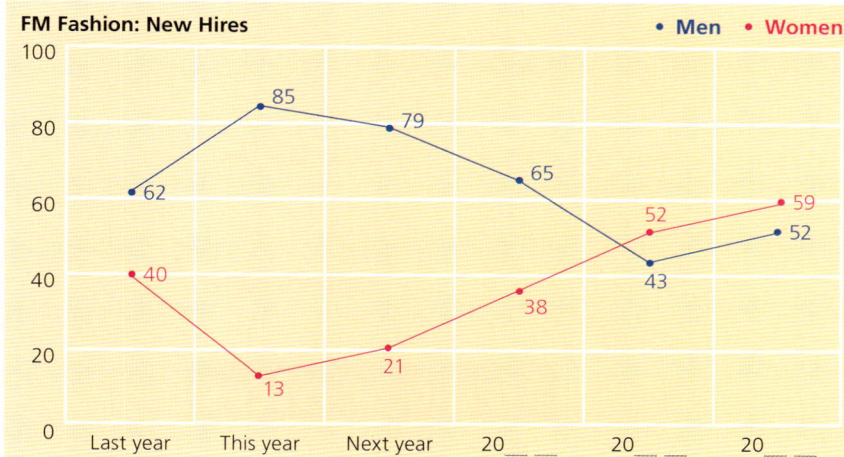

For example:
Q *How many people joined FM Fashion last year?*
A *102.*

FM Fashion: New Hires   • Men   • Women

100
85
80   79
         65
62
60   59
             52
40   52
     40   43
           38
20
     13   21
0
Last year   This year   Next year   20___   20___   20___

For example:
A *38.*
Q *How many women will probably join FM Fashion in 20___?*

6 Don't mention it.

🔘 2.16 Jill wants to thank you. Listen and respond when you hear the beep.

7 I'll definitely climb Mt. Everest!

What are your plans for next year? Complete the sentences. Compare your answers with a partner.

	I'll definitely	
	I'll probably	
Next year	perhaps I'll	
	maybe I'll	

Student A: use this page. (Student B: use page 96)

Useful language			
What	do	you	do?
Who	are do	you	with work for?
What	is	your	address? zip code? phone number? email address?

1 Ask questions to complete student B's business card below. Write B's responses.

Chris Chandler
production _____

_____ **Media Services**
We produce top-quality videos

346 _____ Street
Seattle, Washington _____
(206) 555-_____
_____ @ _____

2 Answer student B's questions about your business card.

PACIFIC FINANCE

Personal Banking Services

Mary Chan
Marketing Manager

105 Thomson Road ... Tel: 6355 5749
33-05 United Square ... Fax: 6355 6763
Singapore 309875
email: chan_c@pacfinance.com

3 Now compare your books. Did you get the correct information?

2 Talk business

Student A: use this page. (Student B: use page 97)

Useful language	
Do you	write emails? take part in one-on-one meetings? take part in teleconferences?
How often do you	give presentations? make telephone calls? go on overseas business trips?

1 Ask student B questions to complete the survey about B's on-the-job use of English. Write B's responses.

Asia Research Center – Survey of on-the-job use of English

ACTIVITY	YES / NO	HOW OFTEN?
read emails		
write emails		
take part in one-on-one meetings		
take part in group meetings		
use the telephone		
take part in teleconferences		
give presentations		
go on overseas business trips		
other: *welcome foreign visitors*		

2 Now answer student B's questions. Use this information.

Asia Research Center – Survey of on-the-job use of English

ACTIVITY	YES / NO	HOW OFTEN?
read emails	Yes	every day
write emails	Yes	every day
take part in one-on-one meetings	Yes	once a month
take part in group meetings	Yes	two or three times a month
use the telephone	Yes	every day
take part in teleconferences	No	–
give presentations	No	–
go on overseas business trips	No	–
other: *give factory tours*	Yes	every month

3 Now compare your books. Did you get the correct information?

3 Talk business

Student A: use this page. (Student B: use page 98)

Useful language				
What	does	your company	do?	
Where	is	your head office?		
When	was	the company	established?	
How many	offices employees	do	you	have?

1 **Ask student B questions to get information about Rock On! Records. Complete the chart.**

Rock On! Records	
Head office:	
Established:	
Employees:	
Offices:	
Factories:	
Business:	

2 **Answer student B's questions about Fujimoto Heavy Industries.**

Fujimoto Heavy Industries	
Head office:	Kawasaki, Japan
Established:	1946
Employees:	32,097
Offices:	Kawasaki, Tokyo, Osaka
Factories:	Kawasaki, Sasebo
Business:	builds ships, makes airplanes

3 **Now compare your books. Did you get the correct information?**

4 Talk business

Student A: use this page. (Student B: use page 99)

Useful language	
You should …	
Why don't you … ?	That's a good idea, thanks.
I recommend …	Well, maybe.
How about … ?	

1 Tell student B your problems. Listen to B's suggestion.

🙂 If you like the suggestion, say, "That's a good idea, thanks."

🙂 If you don't like the suggestion, say, "Well, maybe."

a I feel very sleepy now.
b I don't understand this word.
c I want to buy a cheap plane ticket.
d I usually miss my morning bus.
e I need some more money.

2 Now listen to student B's problems. Make suggestions using the information below.

ride your bicycle to school	go shopping with me
give it to me	try to relax more
read the manual	ask one of your classmates

5 Talk business

Student A: use this page. (Student B: use page 100)

Useful language	
How do you spell (that)?	Can you repeat that?
Can you speak more slowly?	Can you say that again?
Can you speak more loudly?	

1 You are the caller.

You are:	Chris Patterson
At:	J&B Productions
Your phone number is:	077 – 9888 – 6533

Call student B and ask for Jennifer Cho. If she is not there, leave a message. Ask her to call you back tomorrow morning.

Begin the call by saying: *Ring, ring.*

2 You are the receiver.

You will receive a phone call from student B. You are the receptionist for NBI. Ms. Thompson is in a meeting.

Take a message using the form below. Remember to thank the caller and end the phone call!

Telephone Message

To: _margaret Thompson_

From: _____

Tel: _____

Message:

☐ please call back   ☐ other

☐ will call you back

_____
_____
_____
_____

Taken by: _____ **Time:** _____

3 Now compare your books. Did you get the correct information?

Student A: use this page. (Student B: use page 101)

Practice the conversation below. Then have similar conversations using the information in the charts.

A: Do you know which (camera) is (cheaper)?

B: Well, (the XLR) is ($300). How about the (Ricon 900)?

A: That one is ($500).

B: OK, then (the XLR) is (cheaper). You should get that one.

1 Ask shopper B about the PDA, the English book, and the video game.

Begin like this: *Do you know which PDA is lighter?*

1 PDA – light

the Blueberry: ____ grams

the Strawberry: 5 grams

2 English book – short

Great Grammar: ____ pages

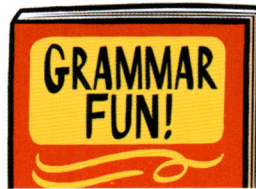

Grammar Fun: 128 pages

3 video game – good

Space Battle: ____ stars

Educational Journey: 2 stars

2 Now talk with shopper B about the suit, the CD, and the ladder. (B starts.)

4 suit – expensive

the Yugo Moss: $900

the Nolo: $____

5 CD – new

Radio Hits: 20 years old

Hot Hip Hop: ____ years old

6 ladder – tall

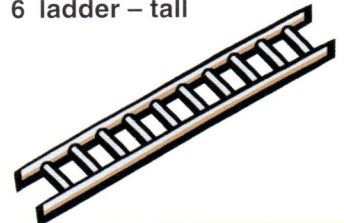

the gray one: 3 meters long

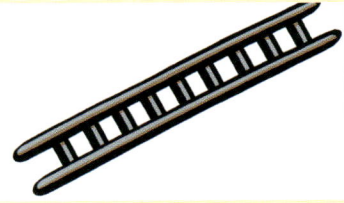

the black one: ____ meters long

3 Now compare your books. Did you get the correct information?

7 Talk business

Student A: use this page. (Student B: use page 102)

Let me confirm. Let me repeat that.	That's … . You said … . The … is … .	Is that right?

---

1 Caller

You are:	Mary Chan

You are calling the Pacific Restaurant. You want to make a lunch reservation.

Restaurant: (Student B)

You: Hello, I'd like to make a reservation, please.

This is your reservation information:

12:45 Pacific Restaurant   Dec 14th

⑤ adults, 3 children

Cell phone: 075 3333 8570

---

2 Receiver

You are:	Anna Martinez
At:	BL Chemicals

You will receive a phone call from Jung-hee Kim at Pusan Pipe. Write down his order in the space below. (Remember to check the information!)

You: Hello, BL Chemicals. How can I help you?

Jung-hee: (Student B)

You: Certainly. Can you give me the part numbers and quantity, Mr. Kim?

Jung-hee: …………

BL Chemicals: Order Form	
Part Number	Quantity

You: Thank you for your order, Mr. Kim. I will send you an email today to confirm this information.

---

3 Now compare your books. Did you get the correct information?

Student A: use this page. (Student B: use page 103)

Useful language	across from behind between in front of
Where is the _____ ?	in the corner next to / on the left
It's …	next to / on the right under

1 Look at the map of the shopping mall below. Ask student B where these stores are, and write them onto the map: *ice cream shop, video game arcade, furniture store, cosmetics store.*

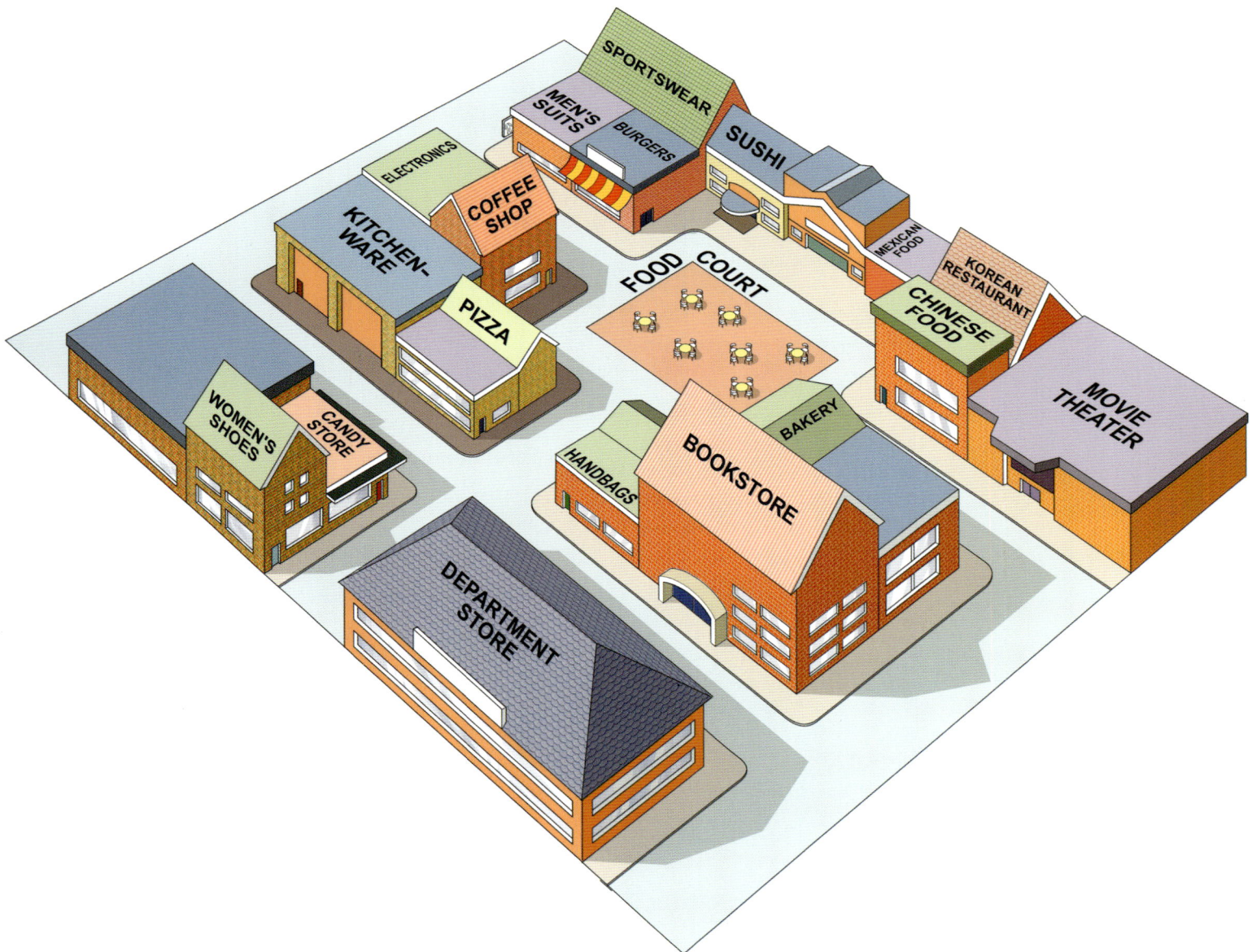

2 Answer student B's questions.

3 Now compare your books. Did you get the right information?

Student A: use this page. (Student B: use page 104)

1 Describe the first part of the process to student B. Check that he / she understands.

Begin like this:
The first step is to research the company.
For example, what are their products? …

Useful language

Is that clear (so far)?
Are you with me (so far)?
OK?

Preparing for a job interview.

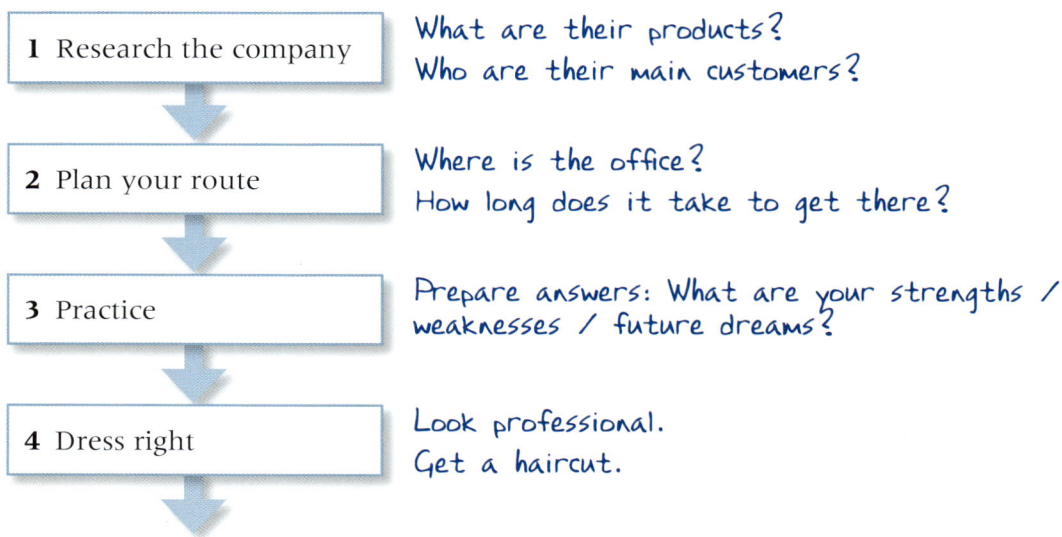

1 Research the company

What are their products?
Who are their main customers?

2 Plan your route

Where is the office?
How long does it take to get there?

3 Practice

Prepare answers: What are your strengths /
weaknesses / future dreams?

4 Dress right

Look professional.
Get a haircut.

2 Now listen to student B's description and complete the second part of the process. Check and confirm that you understand.

Useful language

Yes, that's clear. I understand. I'm with you. OK.	Let me confirm … Let me repeat that …

5 _____ early

_____ _____ minutes early.
_____ off your cell phone.

6 _____ _____ shy!

Talk about your experiences.
_____ _____ who you are!

7 _____ _____

Ask about the company and _____ _____ .
Ask about _____ plans.

8 Follow-up

_____ _____ : Send a thank-you note or _____ .

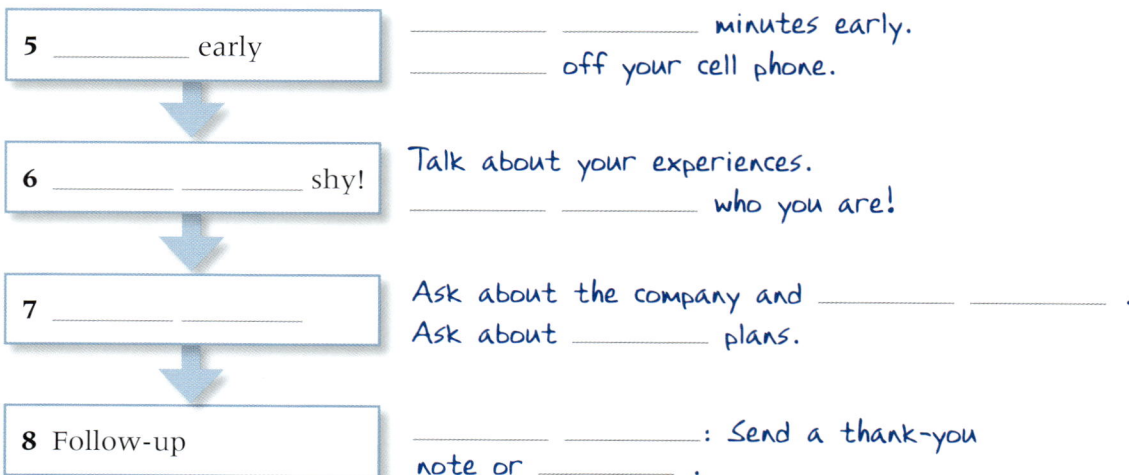

3 Now compare your books. Did you get the correct information?

Student A: use this page. (Student B: use page 105)

Here is information about visitors to the Grand Canyon in Arizona, U.S.

1 **a** **Complete the pie chart. Ask student B for information like this:**

What percentage of visitors to the Grand Canyon were (…)?

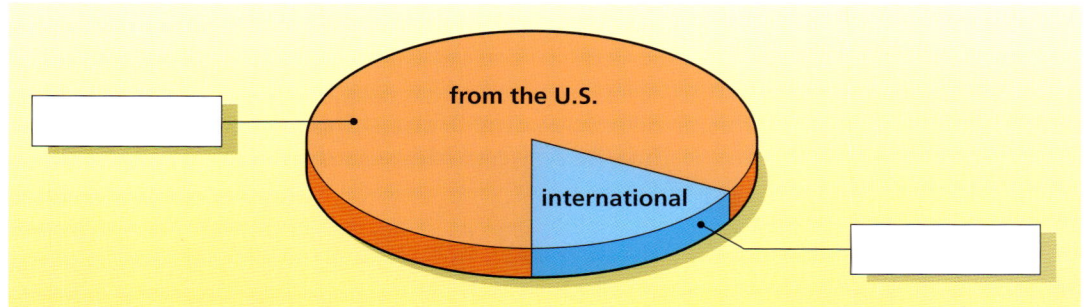

from the U.S.

international

b **Complete the bar graph by drawing in the correct bars for each country. Ask student B for information like this:**

How many people came from (…)?

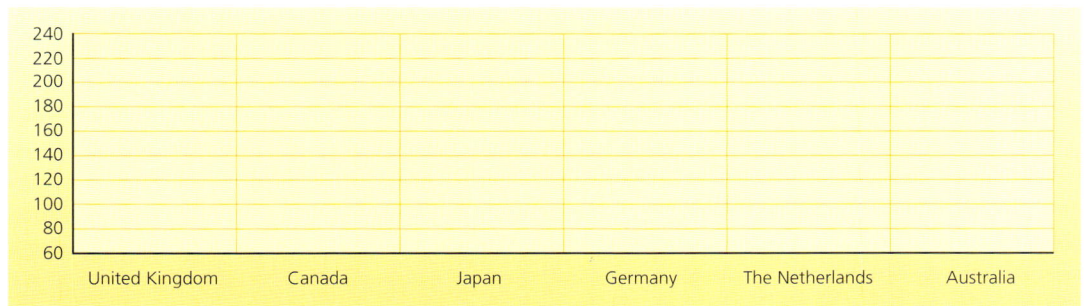

| | United Kingdom | Canada | Japan | Germany | The Netherlands | Australia |

2 **Now answer student B's questions with this information:**

a Most visitors to the Grand Canyon National Park, 58.6 percent, were first-time visitors. 41.4 percent were repeat visitors, or visitors who had been to the park before.

b

State	Number of visitors
California	739
Arizona	535
Texas	288
Florida	204
New York	195
Ohio	190

3 **Now compare your books. Did you get the correct information?**

Student A: use this page. (Student B: use page 106)

(Student B: use page 106)

Useful language	
From January to February we In March we	will … are going to … plan to … hope to …

1 **Describe the development schedule to student B. Check that he / she understands.**

Project XPII – Development Schedule

Time Frame		Action / Event
March – July	▷	Design the parts
July – September	▷	Build a prototype
August – October	▷	Test the prototype
October – November	▷	Contact suppliers
December	▷	Decide on a supplier
January	▷	Plan the production schedule
February	▷	Start production

2 **Listen to student B's description and complete the chart. Remember to confirm that you understand.**

	A	M	J	J	A	S	O	N	D	J	F	M	A	M	J
Advertise (website)	▬														
Colleges / Universities															
Career Fairs															
Group Interviews															
One-on-one Interviews															
Job Offers							▬	▬							
New Hire Orientation															
New Hire Training															

3 **Now compare your books. Did you get the correct information?**

12 Talk business

Student A: use this page. (Student B: use page 107)

Useful language	
A: Would you like a / some (___)?	**B:** Sure. Where is it / are they from?
A: It's / They're from (___).	**B:** What's in it / them?
A: (___).	**B:** Thank you. It looks / They look delicious.

1 Offer student B these dishes. Answer B's questions.

a summer rolls	**b gravlax (on bread)**	**c harira**
summer rolls, Vietnam rice noodles, shrimp, vegetables	**gravlax, Norway** salmon (fish), salt and sugar, mustard, bread	**harira, Morocco** lamb, tomatoes, beans, spices

2 Now student B will offer you these dishes. Ask where they are from and what is in them. Then accept the offer.

d shepherd's pie	**e pavlova**	**f pakoras**

Student B: use this page. (Student A: use page 84)

Useful language			
What	do	you	do?
Who	are do	you	with work for?
What	is	your	address? zip code? phone number? email address?

---

1   Answer student A's questions about your business card.

Chris Chandler
production assistant

Northwest Media Services

We produce top-quality videos

346 Linden Street
Seattle, Washington 98103
(206) 555-9714
c_chand@nwmedia.net

---

2   Now ask questions to complete student A's business card below. Write A's responses.

PACIFIC FINANCE

Personal Banking _____

Mary Chan

_____

105 Thomson Road ... Tel: 6355 5749
_____ United Square ... Fax: 6355 _____
Singapore _____
email: _____@_____

---

3   Now compare your books. Did you get the correct information?

2 | Talk business

Student B: use this page. (Student A: use page 85)

Useful language	
Do you	write emails? take part in one-on-one meetings? take part in teleconferences?
How often do you	give presentations? make telephone calls? go on overseas business trips?

1 Answer student A's questions. Use this information.

Asia Research Center – Survey of on-the-job use of English

ACTIVITY	YES / NO	HOW OFTEN?
read emails	Yes	every day
write emails	Yes	once a week
take part in one-on-one meetings	No	–
take part in group meetings	Yes	once a month
use the telephone	No	–
take part in teleconferences	No	–
give presentations	Yes	every month
go on overseas business trips	Yes	twice a year
other: *welcome foreign visitors*	Yes	three or four times a year

2 Now ask student A questions to complete the survey about A's on-the-job use of English. Write A's responses.

Asia Research Center – Survey of on-the-job use of English

ACTIVITY	YES / NO	HOW OFTEN?
read emails		
write emails		
take part in one-on-one meetings		
take part in group meetings		
use the telephone		
take part in teleconferences		
give presentations		
go on overseas business trips		
other: *give factory tours*		

3 Now compare your books. Did you get the correct information?

Student B: use this page. (Student A: use page 86)

Useful language				
What		does	your company	do?
Where		is	your head office?	
When		was	the company	established?
How many	offices employees	do	you	have?

1 **Answer student A's questions about Rock On! Records.**

Rock On! Records	
Head office:	London, U.K.
Established:	1998
Employees:	214
Offices:	London, New York
Factories:	Tokyo, Los Angeles
Business:	produces music

2 **Ask student A questions to get information about Fujimoto Heavy Industries. Complete the chart.**

Fujimoto Heavy Industries	
Head office:	
Established:	
Employees:	
Offices:	
Factories:	
Business:	

3 **Now compare your books. Did you get the correct information?**

Student B: use this page. (Student A: use page 87)

Useful language	
You should …	
Why don't you … ?	That's a good idea, thanks.
I recommend …	Well, maybe.
How about … ?	

1 **Listen to student A's problems. Make a suggestion using the information below.**

shop online	get up earlier
buy a new one	check a dictionary
drink some coffee	get a part-time job

2 **Tell student A your problems. Listen to A's suggestion.**

🙂 If you like the suggestion, say, "That's a good idea, thanks."

🙁 If you don't like the suggestion, say, "Well, maybe."

a I need to buy my friend a gift.
b I can't use my digital camera.
c I don't remember my teacher's name.
d I don't like this shirt.
e I need more exercise.

5 Talk business

Student B: use this page. (Student A: use page 88)

Useful language
How do you spell (that)?
Can you speak more slowly?   Can you repeat that?
Can you speak more loudly?   Can you say that again?

1 You are the receiver.

You will receive a phone call from student A. You are the receptionist for CNS Marketing. Ms. Cho is not at her desk now.

Take a message using the form below. Remember to thank the caller and end the phone call!

Telephone Message

To: _Jennifer Cho_

From: _____

Tel: _____

Message:

☐ please call back   ☐ other

☐ will call you back

_____

_____

_____

_____

Taken by: _____ Time: _____

2 You are the caller.

You are:	Lisa Gomez
At:	Aztec Coffee
Your phone number is:	55 – 5286 – 1397

Call student A and ask for Margaret Thompson. If she is not there, leave a message. Ask her to call you back this afternoon before 5:30.

Begin the call by saying: _Ring, ring._

3 Now compare your books. Did you get the correct information?

6 Talk business

Practice the conversation below. Then have similar conversations using the information in the charts.

A: Do you know which (camera) is (cheaper)?

B: Well, (the XLR) is ($300). How about the (Ricon 900)?

A: That one is ($500).

B: OK, then (the XLR) is (cheaper). You should get that one.

1 Talk with shopper A about the PDA, the English book, and the video game. (A starts.)

1 PDA – light

the Blueberry: 3 grams

the Strawberry: ____ grams

2 English book – short

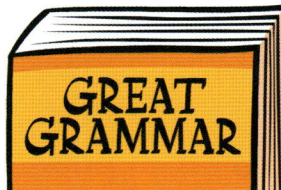

Great Grammar: 380 pages

Grammar Fun: ____ pages

3 video game – good

Space Battle: 5 stars

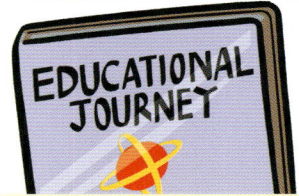

Educational Journey: ____ stars

2 Now ask shopper A about the suit, the CD, and the ladder.
Begin like this: *Do you know which suit is more expensive?*

4 suit – expensive

the Yugo Moss: $____

the Nolo: $2,500

5 CD – new

Radio Hits: ____ years old

Hot Hip Hop: 2 years old

6 ladder – tall

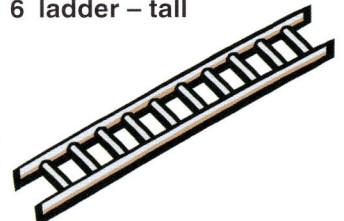

the gray one: ____ meters long

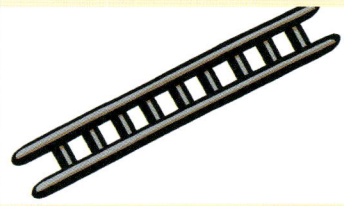

the black one: 2 meters long

3 Now compare your books. Did you get the correct information?

Student B: use this page. (Student A: use page 90)

| Let me confirm. Let me repeat that. | That's ... . You said ... . The ... is ... . | Is that right? |

---

1 Receiver

| You are: | Jenny Sanderson |
| At: | Pacific Restaurant |

You will receive a phone call. Write down the reservation information in the space below. (Remember to check the information!)

You: Good morning, Pacific Restaurant. How can I help you?

Mary: (Student A)

You: Certainly. Can I have your name, please?

Pacific Restaurant: RESERVATION ORDER

GUEST NAME: _____ DATE: _____ TIME: _____

NO. OF PEOPLE: _____ ADULTS: _____ CHILDREN: _____

TEL: _____

You: Thank you for your call. We look forward to serving you.

---

2 Caller

| You are: | Jung-hee Kim |
| At: | Pusan Pipe |

You are calling Anna Martinez at BL Chemicals. You want to order some parts.

Anna: (Student A)

You: Hello, this is Jung-hee Kim at Pusan Pipe. I'd like to order some parts.

Anna: ...

You: Yes, the first one is ...

This is your order:

Need to order from BL Chemicals:

Part No.	Quantity
DD 3245	877
DK 5666Y	2000
YT4176A	619
YT4177D	1500

---

3 Now compare your books. Did you get the correct information?

8 | Talk business

Student B: use this page. (Student A: use page 91)

Useful language	across from behind between in front of
Where is the _____ ?	in the corner next to / on the left
It's …	next to / on the right under

1 Look at the map of the shopping mall below. Answer student A's questions.

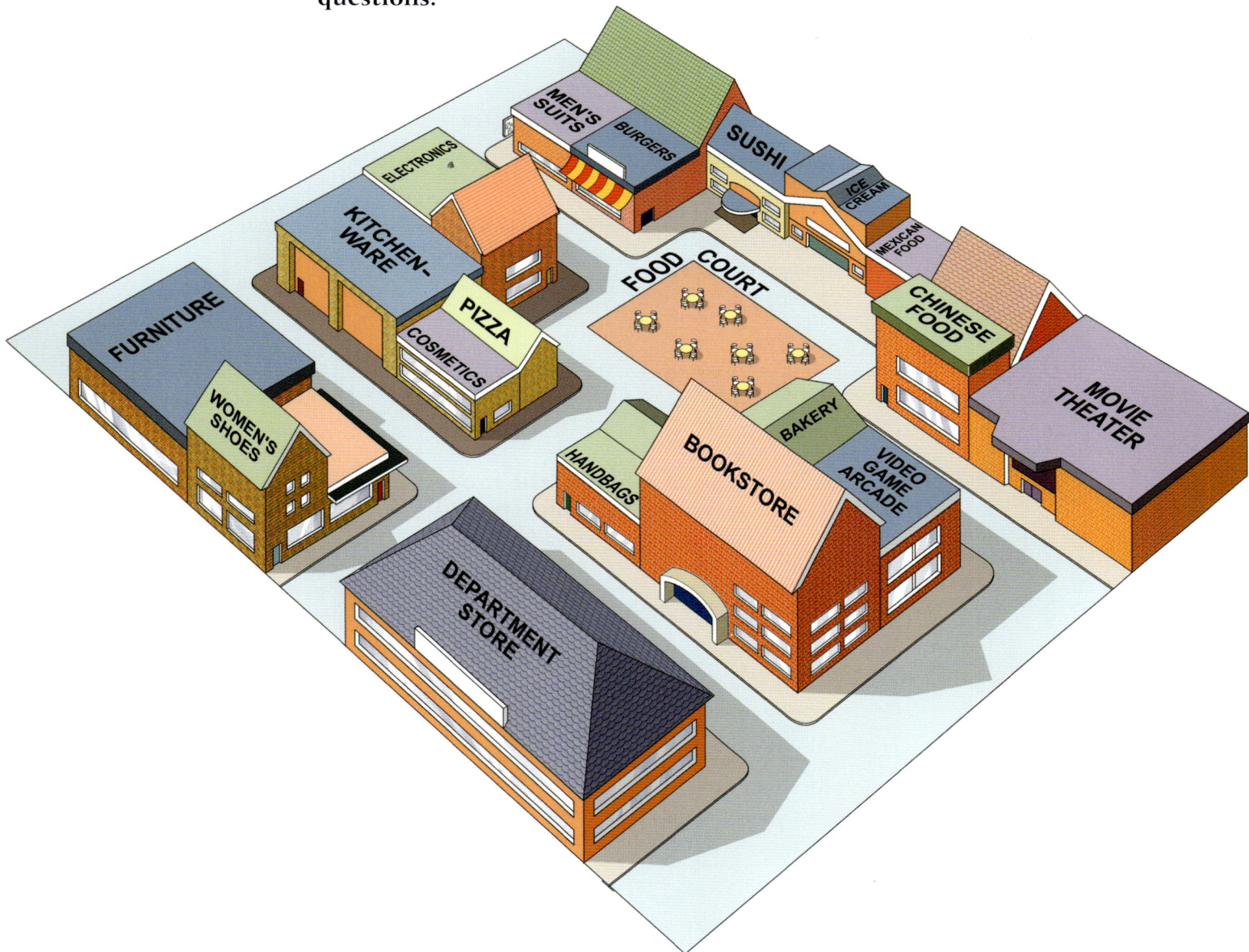

2 Ask student A where these stores are, and write them onto the map: *candy store, sportswear store, Korean restaurant, coffee shop.*

3 Now compare your books. Did you get the correct information?

9 Talk business

Student B: use this page. (Student A: use page 92)

1 **Listen to student A's description and complete the first part of the process. Check and confirm that you understand.**

Useful language	
Yes, that's clear. I understand. I'm with you. OK.	Let me confirm … Let me repeat that …

Preparing for a job interview.

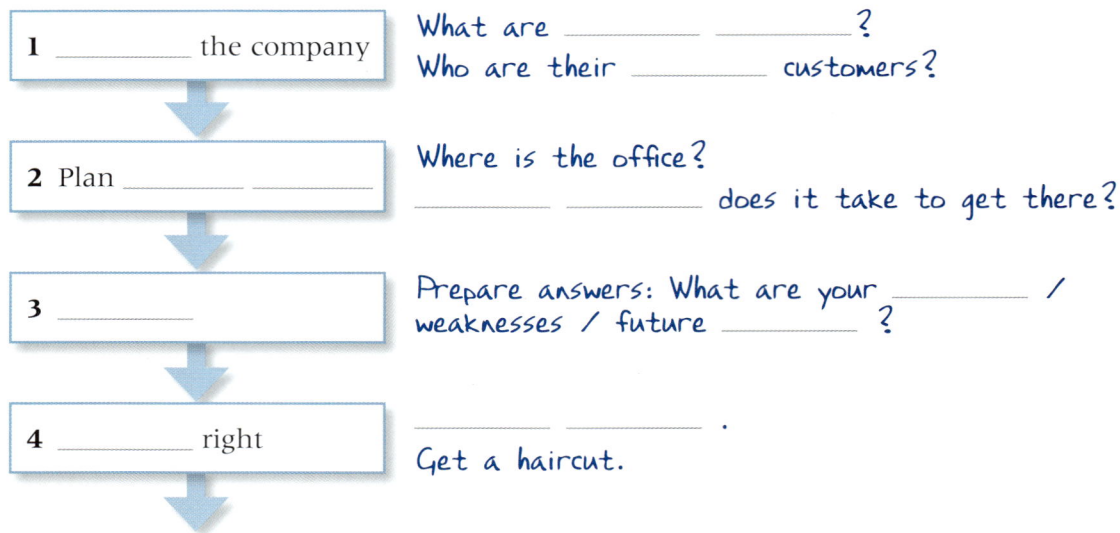

1 _____ the company

What are _____ _____ ?
Who are their _____ customers?

2 Plan _____ _____

Where is the office?
_____ _____ does it take to get there?

3 _____

Prepare answers: What are your _____ /
weaknesses / future _____ ?

4 _____ right

_____ _____ .
Get a haircut.

2 **Now describe the second part of the process to student A. Check that he / she understands.**

Begin like this:
The next step is to arrive early. This means you should be 20 minutes early. …

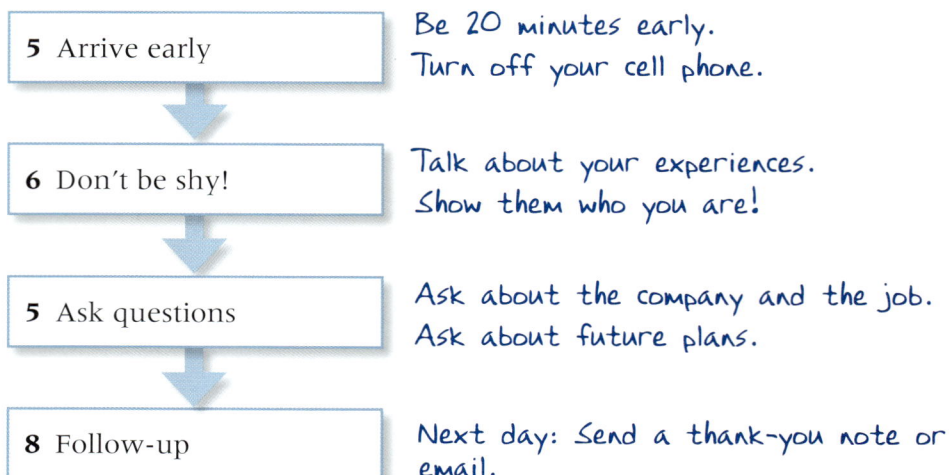

Useful language
Is that clear (so far)? Are you with me (so far)? OK?

5 Arrive early

Be 20 minutes early.
Turn off your cell phone.

6 Don't be shy!

Talk about your experiences.
Show them who you are!

5 Ask questions

Ask about the company and the job.
Ask about future plans.

8 Follow-up

Next day: Send a thank-you note or email.

3 **Now compare your books. Did you get the correct information?**

10 Talk business

Here is information about visitors to the Grand Canyon in Arizona, U.S.

1 Answer student A's questions with this information:

a Most visitors to Grand Canyon National Park, 83 percent, were from the United States. 17 percent of visitors were international.

b

Country	Number of visitors
United Kingdom	227
Canada	209
Japan	129
Germany	117
The Netherlands	71
Australia	65

2 a Now complete the pie chart. Ask student A for information like this:

What percentage of people were (…)?

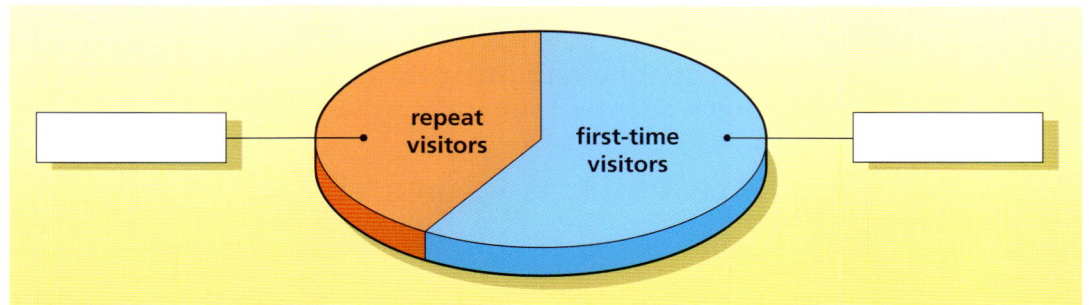

b Complete the bar graph by drawing in the correct bars for each country. Ask student A for information like this:

How many people came from (…)?

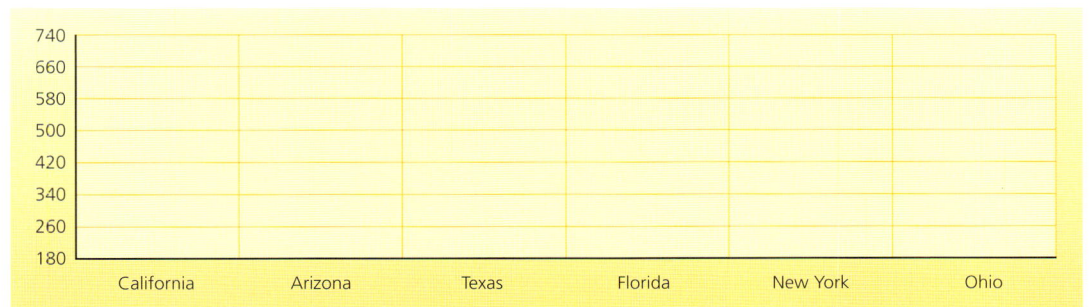

3 Now compare your books. Did you get the correct information?

Student B: use this page. (Student A: use page 94)

Useful language	
From January to February we In March we	will … are going to … plan to … hope to …

1 Listen to student A's description and complete the chart. Remember to confirm that you understand.

	M	A	M	J	J	A	S	O	N	D	J	F
Parts Design												
Prototype												
Testing												
Contact Suppliers								▬	▬			
Decide Supplier												
Production Schedule												
Production												▬

2 Describe the recruiting timeline to student A. Check that he / she understands.

New Hire Recruitment – Timeline

Time Frame		Action / Event
April	▷	Post job openings on the website
May – June	▷	Visit colleges & universities
July	▷	Attend career fairs
July – August	▷	Interview candidates (group)
August – September	▷	Interview candidates (one-on-one)
October – November	▷	Make job offers
April	▷	Give orientation to new hires
April – June	▷	New hire training

3 Now compare your books. Did you get the correct information?

12 Talk business

Student B: use this page. (Student A: use page 95)

Useful language	
A: Would you like a / some (___)?	**B:** Sure. Where is it / are they from?
A: It's / They're from (___).	**B:** What's in it / them?
A: (___).	**B:** Thank you. It looks / They look delicious.

1 Student A will offer you these dishes. Ask where they are from and what is in them. Then accept the offer.

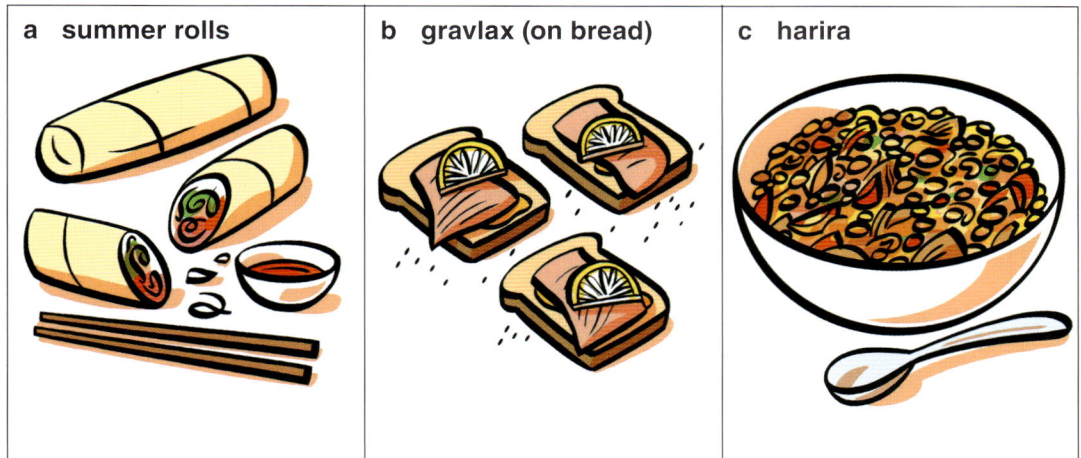

a summer rolls	b gravlax (on bread)	c harira

2 Offer student A these dishes. Answer A's questions.

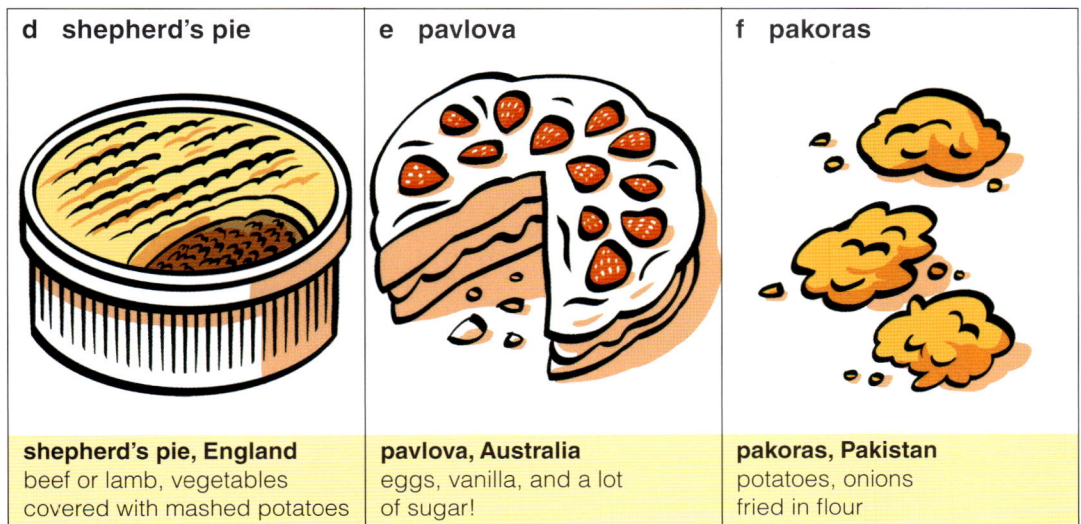

d shepherd's pie	e pavlova	f pakoras
shepherd's pie, England beef or lamb, vegetables covered with mashed potatoes	**pavlova, Australia** eggs, vanilla, and a lot of sugar!	**pakoras, Pakistan** potatoes, onions fried in flour

Unit 1: TOEIC® practice

A Photographs

2.17 **Listen. Then choose the sentence that best describes the photo.**

1 (A) (B) (C) (D)   **2** (A) (B) (C) (D)

B Sentence – Response

2.18 **Listen. Then choose the best response to the sentence you hear.**

3 (A) (B) (C)   **5** (A) (B) (C)

4 (A) (B) (C)   **6** (A) (B) (C)

READING: Sentence completion

Choose the best word to complete each sentence.

7 I'm sorry, I didn't _____ your name.
(A) meet
(B) know
(C) give
(D) catch

8 Well, I'll see you _____ .
(A) with
(B) around
(C) after
(D) ahead

9 What's the country _____ for Germany?
(A) code
(B) hyphen
(C) area
(D) city

10 I'm a sales _____ .
(A) marketing
(B) developer
(C) product
(D) representative

11 I'm _____ purchasing.
(A) at
(B) for
(C) in
(D) on

12 _____ me give you my card.
(A) Tell
(B) Let
(C) See
(D) Hear

Unit 2: TOEIC® practice

LISTENING: Short conversations and talks

🔘 2.19 Listen. Then answer the questions.

1 Who are the speakers?
(A) Strangers meeting each other
(B) A clerk and a customer
(C) Business co-workers
(D) Husband and wife

2 What are they planning to do?
(A) Type an order
(B) Attend a meeting
(C) Make a phone call
(D) Buy a product

3 Where are the speakers?
(A) At a restaurant
(B) At work
(C) At the airport
(D) At a train station

4 What is the woman asking about?
(A) A schedule
(B) A map
(C) A phone call
(D) A watch

5 What is the man talking about?
(A) His company's working hours
(B) His new job schedule
(C) His daily routine
(D) His boss's business trip

6 What time does the meeting start?
(A) 7:00
(B) 7:30
(C) 8:00
(D) 8:30

READING: Passage completion

Read the passage. Choose the best word to complete each sentence.

From:	oliv67@dfsinternet.co.uk	To:	anyab@yahoo.com	Subject:	New job!

Hi Anya,

I started my new job this week. I really like it. I have to get up early, because it starts

_____ 7:30 in the morning! I _____ for coffee and a muffin most days because I don't

7 (A) in
(B) at
(C) on
(D) to

8 (A) stop
(B) try
(C) eat
(D) make

have time to eat at home. We usually _____ a short morning meeting, and then there's a

9 (A) has
(B) have
(C) having
(D) are having

long meeting _____ a week on Fridays. I don't have much work yet because I just

10 (A) every
(B) some
(C) twice
(D) once

started, but I'm sure I'll really like it. I'll email you next week.

See you,

Olivia

Unit 3: TOEIC® practice

LISTENING:

A Photographs

🔘 2.20 Listen. Then choose the sentence that best describes the photo.

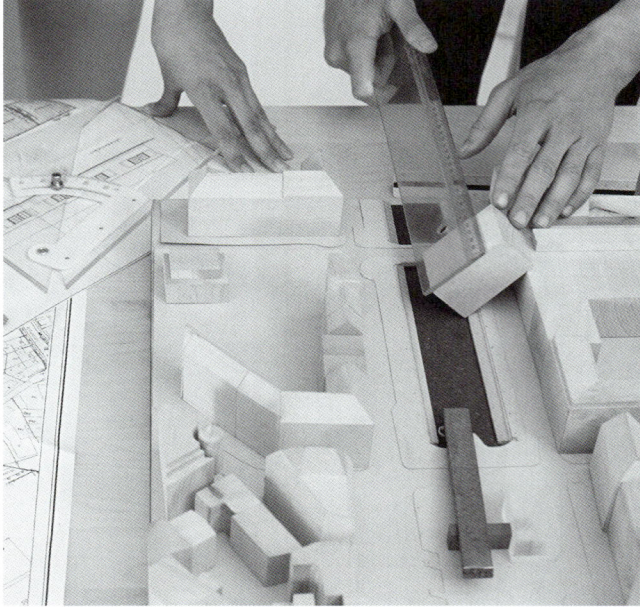

1 (A) (B) (C) (D)   **2** (A) (B) (C) (D)

B Sentence – Response

🔘 2.21 Listen. Then choose the best response to the sentence you hear.

3 (A) (B) (C)   **5** (A) (B) (C)

4 (A) (B) (C)   **6** (A) (B) (C)

READING: Sentence completion

Choose the best word to complete each sentence.

7 Our office has 125 _____ employees.
(A) head
(B) full-time
(C) worker
(D) developed

8 Our company _____ in 2004.
(A) is established
(B) established
(C) was established
(D) were established

9 We have seven factories _____ other countries.
(A) in
(B) at
(C) on
(D) with

10 This company _____ chemical products.
(A) sale
(B) sales
(C) sell
(D) sells

11 Can you _____ your telephone number?
(A) repeat
(B) do
(C) make
(D) ask

12 I _____ work for a small company.
(A) was wanted
(B) want
(C) want to
(D) am wanting

Unit 4: TOEIC® practice

LISTENING: Short conversations and talks

💿 2.22 Listen. Then answer the questions.

1 What does the man think about the woman?
   (A) She looks angry.
   (B) She has good manners.
   (C) She is tired.
   (D) She doesn't work hard.

2 What does the man recommend?
   (A) A vacation
   (B) A shorter schedule
   (C) More training
   (D) A new job

3 What is the woman probably going to do?
   (A) Help her boss with his work
   (B) Go see her manager
   (C) Work on the weekend
   (D) Ask for a day off

4 What is the woman talking about?
   (A) Working overtime
   (B) A company party
   (C) Her personal life
   (D) Her coworkers

5 What time does the event start?
   (A) 6:00 a.m.
   (B) 9:00 a.m.
   (C) 6:00 p.m.
   (D) 9:00 p.m.

6 What does the woman say about food?
   (A) People will pay for their own food.
   (B) They will eat cafeteria food.
   (C) There won't be any food.
   (D) People should recommend food to her.

READING: Reading comprehension

Read the letter. Then answer the questions.

Dear Ms. Morales,

It is my pleasure to write this letter for Victor Hart. I have known Victor for three years. He was my English student last year, and he worked on the student newspaper with me for three years.

   Victor is bright and hard-working. He enjoys challenging subjects and doesn't get frustrated with difficult tasks. His academic work is excellent, and he gets along well with his classmates and has many friends.

   Finally, Victor worked this year as an assistant in the front office. He answered phone calls, typed letters, and helped with general office work. Everyone was pleased with his good work.

   I think Victor would be an excellent student for your university program. Please contact me by phone or email if you have any further questions.

Sincerely,

Matthew J. Lauer

Matthew J. Lauer
English Department
Thomas Jefferson High School

7 What is the purpose of this letter?
   (A) To ask some questions
   (B) To say thank you
   (C) To discuss a problem
   (D) To make a recommendation

8 Who is Matthew J. Lauer?
   (A) A high school student
   (B) A university student
   (C) A high school teacher
   (D) A university professor

9 What does the letter NOT say about Victor?
   (A) He has worked in an office.
   (B) He likes challenging work.
   (C) He wants to study English.
   (D) He is a friendly person.

10 What does Victor want to do?
   (A) Go to a university
   (B) Get a job in an office
   (C) Take a high school class
   (D) Work for a newspaper

Unit 5: TOEIC® practice

LISTENING:

A Photographs

🔊 2.23 **Listen. Then choose the sentence that best describes the photo.**

1 (A) (B) (C) (D)

2 (A) (B) (C) (D)

B Sentence – Response

🔊 2.24 **Listen. Then choose the best response to the sentence you hear.**

3 (A) (B) (C)

4 (A) (B) (C)

5 (A) (B) (C)

6 (A) (B) (C)

READING: Sentence completion

Choose the best word to complete each sentence.

7 I _____ him your message.
(A) give
(B) will give
(C) am giving
(D) giving

8 I'm sorry, I can't _____ you.
(A) listen
(B) speak
(C) talk
(D) hear

9 Just a moment. I'll _____ your call.
(A) transfer
(B) exchange
(C) change
(D) repeat

10 Can you speak more _____ ?
(A) slow
(B) slower
(C) slowly
(D) slowing

11 Ms. Creswell is on another _____ .
(A) message
(B) line
(C) desk
(D) vacation

12 Can you say that _____ ?
(A) another
(B) again
(C) later
(D) out

Unit 6: TOEIC® practice

LISTENING: Short conversations and talks

💿 2.25 **Listen. Then answer the questions.**

1 What are the people talking about?
   (A) A printer
   (B) A watch
   (C) A laptop
   (D) A cell phone

2 Why does the woman like it?
   (A) It's not very expensive.
   (B) She has a coupon for it.
   (C) It's very reliable.
   (D) She wants a large one.

3 What does the man suggest?
   (A) Buying a different one
   (B) Asking for a discount
   (C) Getting a different color
   (D) Buying it later

4 Where could you hear this announcement?
   (A) In a store
   (B) On the radio
   (C) On the phone
   (D) In an office

5 What is the man talking about?
   (A) A sale
   (B) A new model
   (C) A store
   (D) A special service

6 What can you get with the EZ-500?
   (A) A 20% discount
   (B) Free batteries
   (C) A money-back guarantee
   (D) Free shipping

READING: Passage completion

Read the passage. Choose the best word to complete each sentence.

T-shirts, jackets, jeans, shoes, and more, all at great prices!

FASHION WAREHOUSE

This week's specials:

100% _____ men's dress shirts. Buy one, get one _____ !

7 (A) long
   (B) strong
   (C) cotton
   (D) cheap

8 (A) now
   (B) new
   (C) easy
   (D) free

We guarantee that we have _____ prices than any other store in town.

9 (A) better
   (B) good
   (C) more good
   (D) more better

If you're not satisfied, just bring the clothing back for a full _____ .

10 (A) refund
    (B) coupon
    (C) sale
    (D) discount

If you want nicer, _____ clothing, then hurry down to one of our stores.

11 (A) attractive
    (B) more attractive
    (C) kind of attractive
    (D) not so attractive

Or order _____ by visiting our website: http://www.fashionwarehouse.com.

12 (A) on sale
    (B) rather
    (C) actually
    (D) online

Unit 7: TOEIC® practice

LISTENING:

A Photographs

🔘 2.26 **Listen. Then choose the sentence that best describes the photo.**

1 (A) (B) (C) (D)   **2** (A) (B) (C) (D)

B Sentence – Response

🔘 2.27 **Listen. Then choose the best response to the sentence you hear.**

3 (A) (B) (C)   **5** (A) (B) (C)

4 (A) (B) (C)   **6** (A) (B) (C)

READING: Sentence completion

Choose the best word to complete each sentence.

7 I'm free _____ the afternoon.
(A) by
(B) on
(C) at
(D) in

8 I'm calling to _____ my reservation.
(A) confirm
(B) return
(C) order
(D) speak

9 I want to _____ the meeting time.
(A) make
(B) call
(C) change
(D) end

10 Are you free on Tuesday _____ ?
(A) afternoon
(B) the afternoon
(C) early
(D) earlier

11 I'd like _____ a pizza.
(A) order
(B) ordering
(C) to order
(D) ordered

12 Could you ask her to return _____ call?
(A) her
(B) my
(C) him
(D) its

Unit 8: TOEIC® practice

LISTENING: Short conversations and talks

2.28 Listen. Then answer the questions.

1 Where are the speakers?
(A) In a hotel room
(B) At a reception area
(C) On a factory floor
(D) In a bank

2 What does the man want to do?
(A) Make an appointment
(B) Find the stairs
(C) Leave a message
(D) See Ms. Di Angelo

3 Where is the room?
(A) On the 10th floor
(B) Before the stairs
(C) Next to the elevator
(D) Down the hallway to the right

4 Where would you hear this announcement?
(A) On a train
(B) In a movie theater
(C) In a restaurant
(D) At an airport

5 When can you buy something to eat?
(A) In the morning
(B) In fifteen minutes
(C) At 6:00
(D) In half an hour

6 What can you do in the lounge?
(A) Use the telephone
(B) Order a drink
(C) Buy some snacks
(D) Watch a movie

READING: Reading comprehension

Read the email. Then answer the questions.

From:	Mary Allred <mary.allred@goglobal.com>	**To:**	Stephen Parelli <sparelli@newbus.org>
Subject:	Monday's business meeting		

Hi Steve,

I'm glad you can come in on Monday. Let me tell you how to get here.

The easiest way is to take a taxi to the head office. The address is 5216 12th Avenue. It should take about ten minutes. When you walk into the building, you'll see stairs and an elevator on your left. Go up to the 8th floor. When you get out of the elevator, turn left. Our secretary's office is the first room on the right. My office is three doors after that, between the copy room and the stairs.

If you get lost or are going to be late, just call my cell phone.

I look forward to seeing you at 9:30.

Best wishes,
Mary

7 What is the purpose of this email?
(A) To make an appointment
(B) To give directions
(C) To make an introduction
(D) To request some help

8 How do Steve Parelli and Mary Allred know each other?
(A) They work in the same building.
(B) Mary is Steve's secretary.
(C) Steve is applying for a job with Mary.
(D) They are doing business together.

9 Where is the secretary's office?
(A) Next to the stairs
(B) On the 12th floor
(C) Before Mary's office
(D) In front of the elevator

10 How can Steve contact Mary if he has a problem?
(A) By telephone
(B) By talking to her secretary
(C) By email
(D) In person

Unit 9: TOEIC® practice

LISTENING:

A Photographs

🔘 2.29 Listen. Then choose the sentence that best describes the photo.

 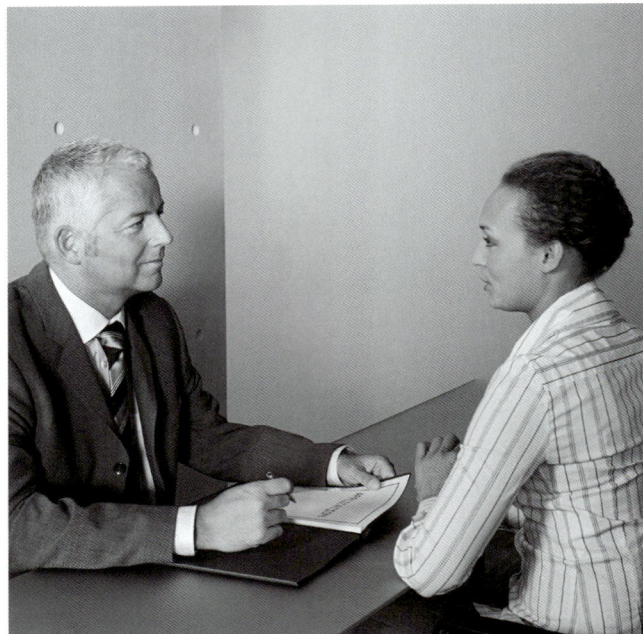

1 (A) (B) (C) (D)   **2** (A) (B) (C) (D)

B Sentence – Response

🔘 2.30 Listen. Then choose the best response to the sentence you hear.

3 (A) (B) (C)   **5** (A) (B) (C)

4 (A) (B) (C)   **6** (A) (B) (C)

READING: Sentence completion

Choose the best word to complete each sentence.

7 The first step is _____ customers.
(A) talk
(B) talking to
(C) talked
(D) to talk

8 _____ the same time, add some water.
(A) To
(B) At
(C) After
(D) In

9 How long does the process _____ ?
(A) be
(B) plan
(C) take
(D) cost

10 Finally, we _____ delivery to our customers.
(A) arrange
(B) enter
(C) send
(D) order

11 Let me _____ sure I understand.
(A) check
(B) see
(C) make
(D) know

12 Is that clear _____ far?
(A) so
(B) too
(C) very
(D) all

Unit 10: TOEIC® practice

LISTENING: Short conversations and talks

🔊 2.31 Listen. Then answer the questions.

1 What does the man want to know?
(A) The delivery schedule
(B) What fax machines to order
(C) How much a product will cost
(D) The date of a meeting

2 What does the woman offer to do?
(A) Find some information
(B) Conduct a training session
(C) Type a document
(D) Hire a new worker

3 What does the man say about her offer?
(A) He wants her to do something different.
(B) He is pleased about it.
(C) He says it isn't necessary.
(D) He doesn't think it will work.

4 What is the speaker doing?
(A) He's checking some data.
(B) He's giving a presentation.
(C) He's developing a plan.
(D) He's training some employees.

5 In what month were sales the highest?
(A) September
(B) October
(C) November
(D) December

6 What does the man suggest that people do next?
(A) Ask any questions they have
(B) Check some information
(C) Go home and come back the next day
(D) Take a short break

READING: Paired reading

Read the chart and letter. Then answer the questions.

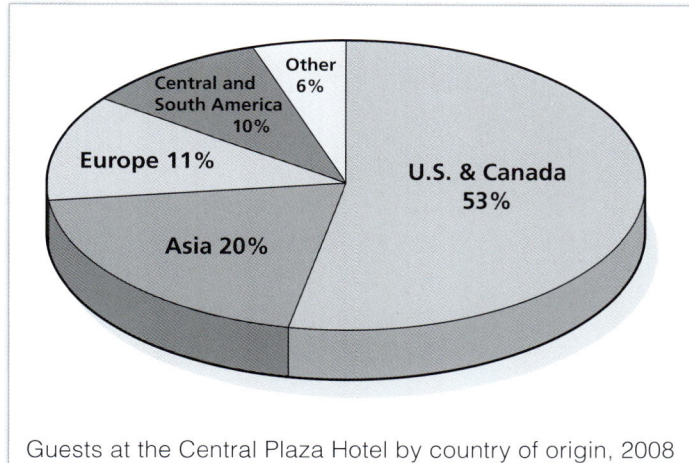

Guests at the Central Plaza Hotel by country of origin, 2008

Dear Frank,

Thank you for meeting with me on Thursday. I'm enclosing a pie chart of the country of origin of our guests. As you can see, most of our guests are from North America, but recently, guests from Asia have increased sharply, probably because of your great advertising campaign.

Now I'd like to do the same for Europe… the number of guests from Europe has remained about the same for the past few years. I'd like to increase that number in 2009. Let's meet again next Thursday at the same time to talk about this.

Best,

Joanne

7 What does the pie chart show?
(A) How many guests stayed at the hotel
(B) How much money the hotel earned
(C) Where the hotel's guests came from
(D) Where the hotel branches are located

8 How many guests come from Europe?
(A) 5%
(B) 10%
(C) 11%
(D) 20%

9 What has increased sharply?
(A) The hotel's profits from guests
(B) The percentage of guests from the U.S. and Canada
(C) The cost of advertising campaigns
(D) The number of guests from Asia

10 What does Joanne want?
(A) To get more guests from Europe
(B) To offer more services at the hotel
(C) To decrease the number of guests from Asia
(D) To charge more money for hotel rooms

Unit 11: TOEIC® practice

LISTENING:

A Photographs

🔘 2.32 Listen. Then choose the sentence that best describes the photo.

1 (A) (B) (C) (D)

2 (A) (B) (C) (D)

B Sentence – Response

🔘 2.33 Listen. Then choose the best response to the sentence you hear.

3 (A) (B) (C)

5 (A) (B) (C)

4 (A) (B) (C)

6 (A) (B) (C)

READING: Sentence completion

Choose the best word to complete each sentence.

7 Please finish the report _____ 6:00.
(A) on
(B) from
(C) by
(D) until

8 I'll work on this _____ away.
(A) right
(B) now
(C) already
(D) just

9 What are you going _____ this afternoon?
(A) do
(B) doing
(C) to do
(D) are doing

10 We're planning to _____ our business.
(A) meet
(B) hire
(C) take
(D) expand

11 In three years, I'll probably _____ a manager.
(A) be
(B) will be
(C) being
(D) am

12 I hope to _____ to a different office.
(A) pack
(B) transfer
(C) arrange
(D) build

Unit 12: TOEIC® practice

LISTENING: Short conversations and talks

2.34 Listen. Then answer the questions.

1 What does the woman ask about?
(A) How to eat enchiladas
(B) Where enchiladas come from
(C) What enchiladas are made from
(D) Who cooked the enchiladas

2 What does the man NOT say is in the enchiladas?
(A) A sauce
(B) Cheese
(C) Vegetables
(D) Beans

3 Why won't the woman eat the enchiladas?
(A) She's on a diet.
(B) She doesn't eat meat.
(C) The food doesn't look good.
(D) She's already eaten some.

4 At what occasion is the man speaking?
(A) A wedding
(B) A business meeting
(C) A birthday party
(D) A family dinner

5 How does the speaker know Joe?
(A) He is Joe's brother.
(B) He and Joe went to the same school.
(C) He hired Joe for a job.
(D) He is Joe's manager at work.

6 What is Joe going to do soon?
(A) Serve food to his guests
(B) Hire more staff at work
(C) Open a new office
(D) Move to another country

READING: Passage completion

Read the passage. Choose the best word to complete each sentence.

Business Entertaining
Focus on Australia

To be successful on your business trip to Australia, follow these tips for mealtimes:

* Keep your hands above the table when you eat. Australians hold the _____ in the left hand and the knife in the right hand.

  7 (A) fork
  (B) sauce
  (C) food
  (D) salad

* If you're invited _____ dinner, come on time. For an informal party, it's OK to be 15 minutes late.

  8 (A) in
  (B) on
  (C) at
  (D) to

* It's polite to _____ something to drink or a small gift if you're invited to someone's home.

  9 (A) have
  (B) bring
  (C) dip
  (D) put

* Barbecues are _____ . Meat is a common _____ served at these outdoor parties.

  10 (A) allergic
  (B) popular
  (C) clever
  (D) kind

  11 (A) plate
  (B) dish
  (C) hand
  (D) diet

* Australians are friendly and casual at mealtimes. Just relax and enjoy the _____ occasion.

  12 (A) socialized
  (B) socialize
  (C) society
  (D) social

* Save business for the office.

Glossary

Unit 1

accountant *(n)*
administrative assistant *(n)*
advertising *(n)*
area code *(n)*
business card *(n)*
construction *(n)*
conversation *(n)*
country code *(n)*
department *(n)*
designer *(n)*
dot *(n)*
email *(v)*
engineer *(n)*
human resources *(n)*
imaginary *(adj)*
information technology *(n)*
limited *(adj)*
logo *(n)*
manager *(n))*
marketing *(n)*
meet *(v)*
planner *(n)*
pretend *(v)*
product *(n)*
purchase *(v)*
researcher *(n)*
sales clerk *(n)*
underscore *(v)*
zip code *(n)*

Unit 2

customer *(n)*
manufacturing *(n)*
married *(adj)*
meeting *(n)*
muffin *(n)*
pass *(n)*
presentation *(n)*
sandwich *(n)*
schedule *(n)*
support *(n)*
teleconference *(n)*
train *(n)*

Unit 3

build *(v)*
design *(v)*
develop *(v)*
employee *(n)*
establish *(v)*
full-time *(adj)*
integrated circuit *(n)*
produce *(v)*
provide *(v)*

Unit 4

advice *(n)*
angry *(adj)*
boring *(adj)*
confusing *(adj)*
corporate *(adj)*
culture *(n)*
custom *(n)*
difficult *(adj)*
earlier *(adj)*
exhausted *(adj)*
frustrating *(adj)*
hiking *(n)*
impolite *(adj)*
manual *(n)*
miss *(v)*
online *(adj)*
paint *(v)*
polite *(adj)*
pretty *(adv)*
situation *(n)*
sleepy *(adj)*
small talk *(n)*
tone *(n)*
training *(n)*

Unit 5

finance *(n)*
message *(n)*
receptionist *(n)*
text message *(n)*
transfer *(v)*

Unit 6

compact *(adj)*
discount *(n)*
display *(v)*
efficient *(adj)*
energy *(n)*
expensive *(adj)*
fashionable *(adj)*
heavy *(adj)*
ladder *(n)*
light *(adj)*
mailing *(n)*
package *(n)*
PDA *(n)*
promise *(v)*
quality *(n)*
refreshing *(adj)*
reliable *(adj)*
scooter *(n)*
script *(n)*
shredder *(n)*
worse *(adj)*

Unit 7

chat *(v)*
complicated *(adj)*
formal *(adj)*
efficient *(adj)*
inefficient *(adj)*
informal *(adj)*
quantity *(n)*
reservation *(n)*
simple *(adj)*

Unit 8

ATM (automated teller machine) *(n)*
cosmetics [plural] *(n)*
drinking fountain *(n)*
elevator *(n)*
furniture *(n)*
hall *(n)*
secretary *(n)*

Unit 9

data *(n)*
delivery *(n)*
feedback *(n)*
flow chart *(n)*
inventory *(n)*
invoice *(n)*
launch *(v)*
layout *(n)*
professional *(adj)*
recruit *(v)*
résumé *(n)*
shy *(adj)*
smoothie *(n)*
strength *(n)*
turn off *(phrasal verb)*
weakness *(n)*

Unit 10

audience *(n)*
atmosphere *(n)*
average *(adj)*
bar graph *(n)*
budget *(n)*
complaint *(n)*
decrease *(v)*
distracting *(adj)*
increase *(v)*
invent *(v)*
joke *(v)*
joke *(n)*
official *(adj)*
pie chart *(n)*
population *(n)*
prime minister *(n)*
sharply *(adv)*
slightly *(adv)*
topic *(n)*
visual aid *(n)*

Unit 11

agenda *(n)*
contract *(n)*
cost *(n)*
estimate *(n)*
expand *(v)*
hire *(v)*
marathon *(n)*
next *(adj)*
overseas *(adv)*
send *(v)*
step *(n)*

Unit 12

accessory *(n)*
allergic *(adj)*
brownie *(n)*
chopstick *(n)*
compliment *(n)*
dip *(v)*
impression *(n)*
hurt (someone's feelings) *(v)*
diet *(n)*
recipe *(n)*
salty *(adj)*
shrimp *(n)*
spicy *(adj)*
vanilla *(n)*
vegetarian *(adj)*

Look it Up

These words are all on the Viewpoints pages (in bold) and the definitions are taken from the *Macmillan English Dictionary* second edition.

All red words have a 'star rating':
★★★ the 2,500 most common and basic English words
★★ very common words
★ fairly common words

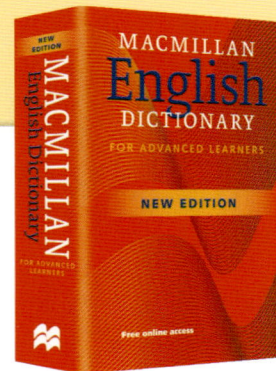

Unit 1

fancy *(adj)* ★
not plain or simple but with a lot of decorations or extra parts

organize *(v)* ★★★
to put things into a sensible order or into a system in which all parts work well together

plain *(adj)* ★★
simple in design, with no decoration

pocket *(n)* ★★★
a small bag that forms part of a piece of clothing and is used for holding small objects

receive *(v)* ★★★
to get something that someone gives or sends to you

respect *(n)* ★★★
a feeling that something is important and deserves serious attention

Unit 2

flexitime *(n)*
a system in which workers choose the hours each day that they work, as long as the hours add up to the same fixed number of hours every week or month
(**American** flextime)

overtime *(n)* ★
extra hours that someone works at their job

property developer *(n)*
someone who earns money by buying land and building on it

telecommuter *(n)*
someone who works from home on a computer and sends work to their office over telephone lines by MODEM or FAX

time off *(n)*
time when you are not at work or at school

vacation *(n)*
a holiday

Unit 3

aerospace *(adj)*
relating to the science or business of building and flying airplanes and space vehicles

automotive *(adj)*
relating to cars

banking *(n)* ★★
the work done by banks and other financial institutions

chemical *(adj)* ★★
involving chemistry or produced by a method used in chemistry

education *(n)* ★★★
the activity of educating people in schools, colleges, and universities, and all the policies and arrangements concerning this

electronics *(n)* ★★
the science and technology that uses or produces electronic equipment

entertainment *(n)* ★★
performances that people enjoy

farming *(n)* ★
the activity or business of being a farmer

fishing *(n)* ★★
the sport or business of catching fish

health care *(n)* ★
the services that look after people's health

hospitality *(n)* ★★
food, drink, and entertainment given to customers by a company or organization

IT *(n)* ★
information technology: the use of computers and other electronic equipment to store, process, and send information

the media *(n)* ★★★
radio, television, newspapers, the Internet, and magazines considered as a group: can be followed by a singular or plural verb

mining *(n)* ★
the process of getting coal or metal from under the ground

news *(n)* ★★★
information about recent events that is reported in newspapers or on television or radio

Definitions from the *Macmillan English Dictionary* 2nd edition published 2007, text © A&C Black Publishers 2007.
www.macmillandictionaries.com

pharmaceutical *(adj)*
relating to the production or sale of medicines and drugs used for treating medical conditions

shipbuilding *(n)*
the industry involved in building ships

software *(n)* ★★★
programs used by computers for doing particular jobs

tourism *(n)* ★★
the business of providing services for people who are travelling for their holiday

transportation *(n)* ★
the activity of moving people or things from one place to another, or the system used for doing this

Unit 4

casual *(adj)* ★★
relaxed and informal

greet *(v)* ★★
to behave in a polite or friendly way towards someone when you meet them

manners [plural] *(n)* ★★★
traditionally accepted ways of behaving that show a polite respect for other people

opinion *(n)* ★★★
the attitude that you have towards something, especially your thoughts about how good it is

praise *(v)* ★★
to express strong approval or admiration for someone or something, especially in public

Unit 5

alarm *(n)* ★★
(an alarm clock: a clock that wakes you up at a particular time by making a noise)

convenient *(adj)* ★★
easy to do, or not causing problems or difficulties

text *(v)*
to send a written message to someone using a mobile phone
(**American** cell phone)

Unit 6

annoyed *(adj)* ★★
feeling slightly angry or impatient

bother *(v)* ★★★
if you do not bother to do something, you do not do it, either because there seems to be no good reason or because it involves too much effort

celebrity *(n)* ★
a famous person, especially in entertainment or sport

competitor *(n)* ★★
a company that sells the same goods or services as another company

endorsement *(n)*
an occasion when someone famous says in an advertisement that they like a product

especially *(adv)* ★★★
used when mentioning conditions that make something more relevant, important, or true

flash *(v)* ★★
to shine brightly for a very short time, or to shine on and off very quickly

image *(n)* ★★★
a photograph, painting, or other work of art that represents a person or thing

interrupt *(v)* ★★
to make something stop for a period of time

Unit 7

chat *(v)* ★★
to exchange messages with someone using a computer so that you are able to see each other's messages immediately, especially on the internet

complicated *(adj)* ★★
difficult to do, deal with, or understand, especially because of involving a lot of different processes or aspects

formal *(adj)* ★★★
following the correct or suitable official methods

efficient *(adj)* ★★★
something that is efficient works well and produces good results by using the available time, money, supplies etc in the most effective way

inefficient *(adj)*
not working in the best possible way, especially by not using time, supplies, energy etc in the most effective way

informal *(adj)* ★★
relaxed and friendly

simple *(adj)* ★★
easy to understand, solve, or do

teleconference *(n)*
a meeting held among people in different places using an electronic communications system, often television

Definitions from the *Macmillan English Dictionary* 2nd edition published 2007, text © A&C Black Publishers 2007.
www.macmillandictionaries.com

Unit 8

clinic *(n)* ★★
a place where people go to receive a particular type of medical treatment or advice

convenience store *(n)*
a small shop that is open for long hours and sells a variety of goods, especially food and drink, cleaning materials, and newspapers or magazines

facility *(n)* ★★★
something such as a room or piece of equipment that is provided at a place for people to use

flexible *(adj)* ★★
able to make changes or deal with a situation that is changing

insurance *(n)* ★★★
an arrangement in which you regularly pay an **insurance company** an amount of money so that they will give you money if something you own is damaged, lost, or stolen, or if you die or are ill or injured

laundry *(n)* ★
a business that washes and irons clothes

pharmacy *(n)*
a shop where medicines are prepared and sold

shift *(n)* ★★
a period of work time in a factory, hospital, or other place where some people work during the day and some work at night

vending machine *(n)*
a machine that you can buy things from, for example cigarettes, sweets, or drinks
(**American** candy)

yoga *(n)*
an activity that involves doing physical and breathing exercises to make you stronger and make your mind and body relax

Unit 9

graduate *(v)* ★
to complete your studies at a university or college, usually by getting a **degree**

internship *(n)*
a job that a student or someone who has recently obtained a degree takes in order to get experience

recommend *(v)* ★★★
to say that someone or something is good and worth using, having, or experiencing

Unit 10

slide *(n)* ★★
a small piece of film in a frame, that you shine light through in order to show the image on a screen

Unit 11

continue *(v)* ★★★
to keep doing something without stopping

Unit 12

appreciate *(v)* ★★
to recognize the good or special qualities of a person, place, or thing

communal *(adj)* ★
owned or used by everyone in a group, especially a group of people who live in the same building

entertain *(v)* ★★
to receive someone as a guest and give them food and drink or other forms of enjoyment

left-handed *(adj)*
someone who is left-handed is born with a natural tendency to use their left hand to do things, especially things such as writing

social *(adj)* ★★★
relating to activities that involve being with other people, especially activities that you do for pleasure

traditional *(adj)* ★★★
relating to or based on very old customs, beliefs, or stories

Common irregular verbs

Here is a list of common irregular verbs in English with their past tense (*I took the test*) and past participle (*I have taken three tests this month*).

Base form	Simple past	Past participle	Base form	Simple past	Past participle
be	was/were	been	make	made	made
become	became	become	meet	met	met
begin	began	begun	pay	paid	paid
break	broke	broken	put	put	put
bring	brought	brought	read	read	read
buy	bought	bought	ride	rode	ridden
catch	caught	caught	run	ran	run
choose	chose	chosen	say	said	said
come	came	come	see	saw	seen
cost	cost	cost	sell	sold	sold
cut	cut	cut	send	sent	sent
do	did	done	show	showed	shown
draw	drew	drawn	sing	sang	sung
drink	drank	drunk	sit	sat	sat
drive	drove	driven	sleep	slept	slept
eat	ate	eaten	speak	spoke	spoken
fall	fell	fallen	spend	spent	spent
feel	felt	felt	stand	stood	stood
find	found	found	swim	swam	swum
fly	flew	flown	take	took	taken
forget	forgot	forgotten	teach	taught	taught
get	got	gotten	tell	told	told
give	gave	given	think	thought	thought
go	went	gone	throw	threw	thrown
have	had	had	understand	understood	understood
hear	heard	heard	wear	wore	worn
know	knew	known	win	won	won
leave	left	left	write	wrote	written
lose	lost	lost			

Macmillan Education
4 Crinan Street
London N1 9XW
A division of Macmillan Publishers Limited
Companies and representatives throughout the world

ISBN: 978-0-2300-3979-7

MACMILLAN LANGUAGEHOUSE LTD., TOKYO
ISBN: 978-4-7773-6325-4

Text © Andrew Vaughan & Dorothy E. Zemach 2008
Design and illustration ©Macmillan Publishers Limited 2008

First published 2008

Designed by Design Collective
Page make-up by Carolyn Gibson
Illustrated by Asa Andersson, Beach, Kaneko & Yuzuru-
Thorogood.net, Yane Christensson, Peter Harper,
Sarah Nayler, Simon Stephenson, Yuzuru Takasaki and
Graham White
Cover design by Design Collective
Cover photographs: **Alamy**/alt.PIX Pte Ltd (l);
Getty Images (r), (m)

The authors and publishers are grateful for permission to
reprint the following copyright material:
Statistics from 'Grand Canyon National Park Northern Arizona:
Tourism Study.' By the Arizona Hospitality Research and
Resource Center. April 2005. Reprinted with permission.

Extracts from the *Macmillan English Dictionary* second edition
published 2007, text © A&C Black Publishers 2007, reprinted by
permission of the publishers.

These materials may contain links for third party websites. We
have no control over, and are not responsible for, the contents of
such third party websites. Please use care when accessing them.

The authors wish to extend their thanks to all those who
contributed to this book with their generous advice and
assistance. We would especially like to thank our colleagues,
management, and students (past and present) at Sumitomo
Electric Industries, Sumitomo Metal Industries, Sumikin-
Intercom, and other companies, for giving us the experience
we needed and for trying out many of the ideas in this book.

For assistance with information about international business
customs, cross-cultural communication, and the TOEIC: Brett
Berquist, Tammy Gilbert, Peiya Gu, Alan Headbloom, Lewis
Lansford, Shinji Okumura, Bruce Rogers, Jaimie Scanlon, Tadao
Seo, Lynn Stafford-Yilmaz, Kelly Tavares, Gregg Stevens, Kay
Westerfield, Tatyana Yahkontova

Thanks to everyone at Macmillan for their support and guidance
in the development of this book. Special thanks to Frances
Lowndes for commissioning the course, and to Marc Goozée, Joe
Wilson, and Carole Hughes for their development and editing of
the manuscript.

Finally – thanks to our families for their patience and support:
Hiroko, Sarah, and Thomas Vaughan; and Will and Sebastian
Mitchell.

TOEIC ® is a registered trademark of Educational Testing Service
(ETS). This publication is not endorsed or approved by ETS.

The test questions and other testing information herein are
provided in their entirety by Macmillan Publishers.

The authors and publishers would like to thank the following
for permission to reproduce their photographs: **Alamy Images**
p62tl; Alamy/ PanaromaMedia p.47(r); **Art Directors and Trip**
p10(tm); **Bananastock** pp16(tl), 16(r), P22(tm), 25(r), 25(l),
27(tm),28(m), 36(tr), 40, 42(tr), 46(l), 62(tm), 68(tm), 80(tr),
112(l), 34(r), 46(r), 80(breakfast), 80(watching TV), 80(party);
Corbis p114(r); **Digital Vision** pp28(r), 62(tr), 62(r); **Getty
Images/Stone/Siri Stafford** p80tl; **Image Source** pp10(tl),
10(tr), P22(tr), 16(tm), 36(tm), 42(tl), 42(tm), 47(l), 54(tm),
54(tr), 68(tl), 68(tr), 108(l), 110(l), 110(r), 112(r), 114(l);
116(r) 118(r), 22(br), 34(l), 80(sports); **istock/Tatian popova**
p8; **Photodisc** p99; **Photolibrary.com** p28(tl); **Photoalto**
p87; **Punchstock** pp22(bm), P22(tl), 80(tm); 80(dessert),
80(unhappy), 81; **Stockbyte** pp22(bl), 108(r), 116(l), 118(l);
Thinkstock pp36(tl), 54(tl).

Although we have tried to trace and contact copyright holders
before publication, in some cases this has not been possible. If
contacted we will be pleased to rectify any errors or omissions at
the earliest opportunity.

Printed and bound in Thailand
2018   2017   2016   2015
14   13   12   11   10